CW01617638

European Computer Driving Licence®

ECDL Advanced

Syllabus 2.0

Module AM3 - Word Processing

Using Microsoft® Word 2003

Release ECDL224v1

Published by:

CiA Training Ltd
Business & Innovation Centre
Sunderland Enterprise Park
Sunderland SR5 2TA
United Kingdom

Tel: +44 (0) 191 549 5002
Fax: +44 (0) 191 549 9005

E-mail: info@ciatraining.co.uk
Web: www.ciatraining.co.uk

ISBN-13: 978 1 86005 649 9

This training, which has been approved by ECDL Foundation, includes exercise items intended to assist Candidates in their training for an ECDL Certification Programme. These exercises are not ECDL Foundation certification tests. For information about authorised Test Centres in different national territories, please refer to the ECDL Foundation website at www.ecdl.org

First published 2009

Downloading the Data Files

The data associated with these exercises must be downloaded from our website. Go to: ***www.ciatraining.co.uk/data***. Follow the on screen instructions to download the appropriate data files.

By default, the data files will be downloaded to **My Documents\CIA DATA FILES\Advanced ECDL\AM3 Word 2003 Data**.

If you prefer, the data can be supplied on CD at an additional cost. Contact the Sales team at ***info@ciatraining.co.uk***.

Aims

To demonstrate the ability to use a word processing application on a personal computer.

To understand and accomplish more advanced operations associated with the editing, layout and organisation of a word processed document and the use of various elements and special tools.

To demonstrate some of the more advanced features, including creating master documents, referencing, working with templates, styles, tables, forms, linking and embedding, editing mail merge documents, creating macros and using automatic formatting.

Objectives

After completing the guide the user will be able to:

- Apply advanced text, paragraph, column and table formatting. Convert text to a table and vice versa.
- Work with referencing features like footnotes, endnotes and captions. Create tables of contents, indexes and cross references.
- Enhance productivity by using fields, forms and templates.
- Apply advanced mail merge techniques and work with automation features like macros.
- Use linking and embedding features to integrate data.
- Collaborate on and review documents. Work with master documents and subdocuments. Apply document security features.
- Work with watermarks, sections and headers and footers in a document.

Assessment of Knowledge

At the end of this guide is a section called the **Record of Achievement Matrix**. Before the guide is started it is recommended that the user completes the matrix to measure the level of current knowledge.

Tick boxes are provided for each feature. **1** is for no knowledge, **2** some knowledge and **3** is for competent.

After working through a section, complete the matrix for that section and only when competent in all areas move on to the next section.

Contents

Section 1
Working Efficiently

By the end of this Section you should be able to:

Appreciate Design Considerations

Recognise Different Techniques That Are Available

Create and Use Hyperlinks

Save Documents in Various Formats

To gain an understanding of the above features, work through the **Driving Lessons** in this **Section**.

For each **Driving Lesson**, read the **Park and Read** instructions, without touching the keyboard, then work through the numbered steps of the **Manoeuvres** on the computer. Complete the **Revision Exercise(s)** at the end of the section to test your knowledge.

Driving Lesson 1 - Design

Park and Read

Whilst any course on advanced word processing applications needs to describe and explain the techniques necessary to produce successful documents, thought should always be given to overall purpose of the finished document and to the intended target audience.

Purpose

Every document produced has a purpose. Before starting to create a document, take some time to consider the purpose behind it and plan the content and style accordingly.

Example 1. Assume you are creating a CV. Its purpose is to communicate to a potential employer the relevant features of your qualifications and experience in an easily accessible format. The style may vary depending on the type of job involved, but the content is almost predetermined. Because of the purpose, the information will probably be summarised and presented in list or table form rather than in a rambling free-form letter.

Example 2. You are creating a poster to advertise a future event for your club or society. Its purpose will be to catch people's eye and to communicate key details of the event, such as content, location and date. So make sure your document is both eye catching and includes all relevant details accurately.

Example 3. You are writing documentation for a new IT system. You must know the purpose of the documentation before starting it. Is it to guide users through its operation, or is it to describe the technical specification so that IT staff can maintain it? Each purpose would result in a completely different document.

Audience

The intended audience can have a major impact on both the content and style of the final document, e.g. a report on company performance may be different if intended for the general staff, or for the Financial Director, and a letter to a friend would look different to a business letter to a customer.

With technical content you should also be aware of the level of knowledge the audience has of the subject and plan the document accordingly. Too much explanation of areas with which the audience is familiar may cause them to lose interest. Likewise, too little explanation for an audience with little or no subject knowledge may have the same effect.

Data sources

Word allows complex documents to contain information drawn from a wide variety of sources, e.g. embedded spreadsheets and charts, database tables as merge sources, images from libraries. When planning your document, make sure you consider the availability and accuracy of all such sources.

Driving Lesson 1 - Continued

Other Considerations

The final form of your document may also affect its style. A printed report may reasonably contain a large amount of detail, possibly divided with headings and subheadings. If the same data is to become the content for a web page or presentation, it would probably need to be more summarised, with more bullet points and visual content.

There may also be other practical considerations to take into account. You might be asked to produce a one page summary or a 1000 word report. Such restrictions would obviously have a major effect on your document plan.

Manoeuvres

1. Look at the two warning notices below. The road safety poster is aimed at children, the entry regulations are for trained technical staff.
2. Consider the purpose and audience for the two notices and how these factors have affected the style and content.
3. Think how effective the posters would be if the styles were reversed.

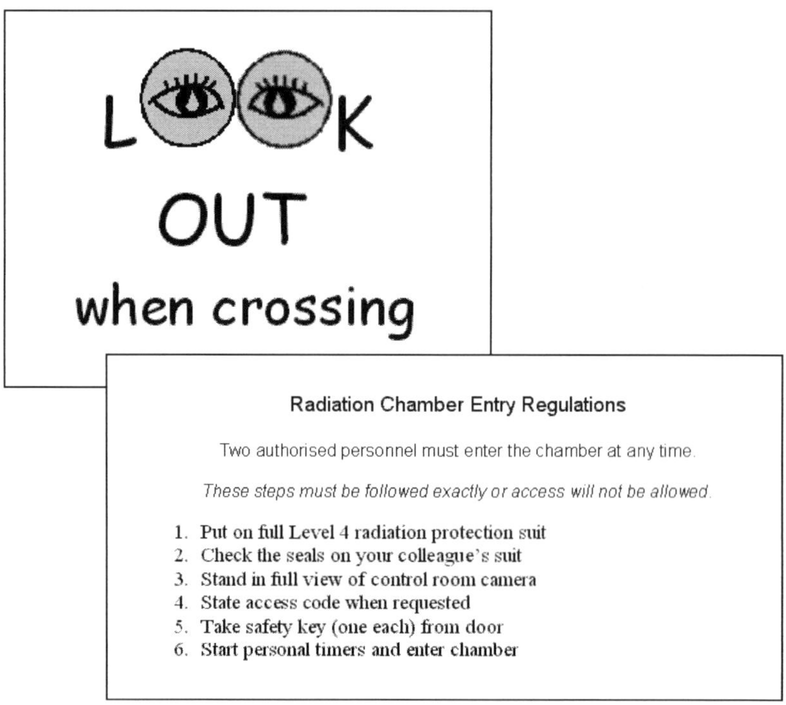

Driving Lesson 3 - Continued

6. Move to the last sentence of the last page of the document, highlight the word **here**, and click **Insert Hyperlink**, .

7. Make sure **Place in This Document** is selected from the left of the dialog box, and if necessary click the ⊞ at the left of **Bookmarks** to reveal the list of available bookmarks.

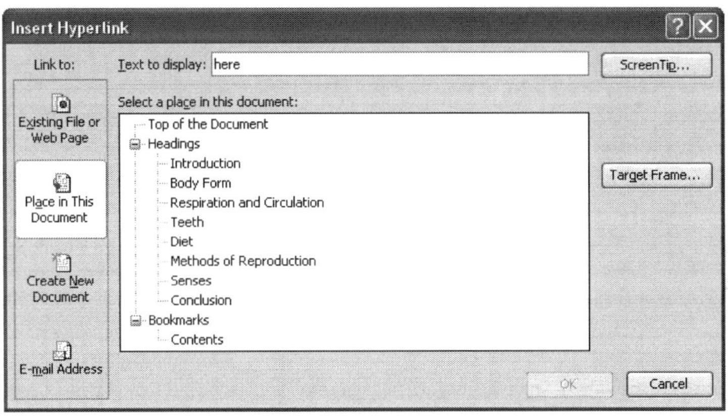

By default you can hyperlink to headings and the top of the document.

8. Select **Contents** and click **OK**. The hyperlink is applied.

9. Click on the word **here** with the <**Ctrl**> key held down to move to the **Contents** bookmark.

10. Move to page 2 and click to select the **shark** image. Click **Insert Hyperlink**, and select **Existing File or Web Page**.

11. You can browse to locate any file or web page on your system to be the target of your hyperlink, or you can type a value into **Address**. For this exercise type **www.ciatraining.co.uk** and click **OK** to insert the hyperlink.

12. Click anywhere on the **shark** image with the <**Ctrl**> key held down to open the **CiA Training** web page (if you have an live Internet connection).

13. Close your browser, and click on the **shark** image to select it. Existing hyperlinks can be amended.

14. Click **Insert Hyperlink**, . The **Edit Hyperlink** dialog box is displayed. Change the **Address** to **www.ciasupport.co.uk** and click **OK**.

15. Test the link then close the browser.

16. Right click on the shark image (or any other hyperlink text) and select **Remove Link**. The hyperlink is removed.

17. Close the **Links** document without saving.

Driving Lesson 4 - Saving

Park and Read

Although the usual format for saving documents is as a **Word Document** (with a **.doc** extension), it is possible to save them in many different formats. One file type is **Plain Text** (with a **.txt** file extension). This means that all formatting, styles and graphics are removed, reducing the file to the simplest text format, making it much smaller and recognisable by most other applications. To save in a format that can be read by any version of *Word*, but still keeps some of the original formatting, save in **Rich Text Format** (**.rtf** file extension). To enable a document to be viewed as a web page, it can be saved in **.htm** format. The location of saved files can also be specified.

Manoeuvres

1. Open the supplied data file **Links2**. This is a multi page document that has had a table of contents and hyperlinks created.
2. Select **File | Save As**.
3. Select a different save location, i.e. not the original folder for the file. Use the **Create New Folder** button, , to create a new folder if you wish. Make a note of the new location.
4. Change the **File name** to **Links3**.
5. Click the drop down arrow from the **Save as type** box and view the various options and their file name extensions. Select **Plain Text (*.txt)**.

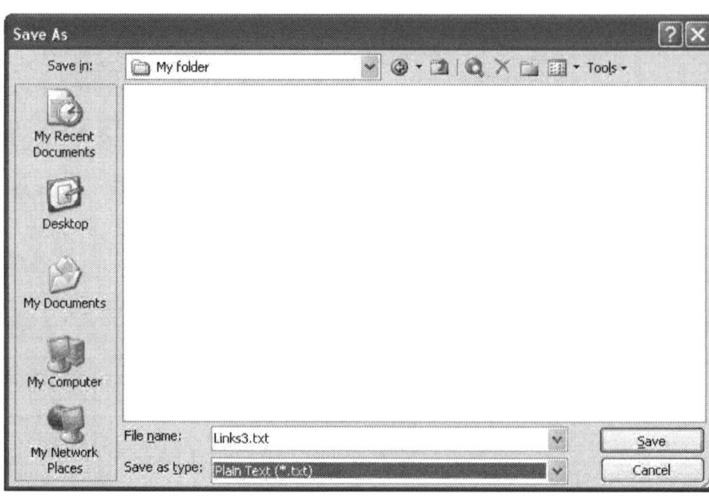

*Saving the File to a new folder **(My folder)***

Driving Lesson 4 - Continued

6. Click **Save**. If a dialog box appears warning about loss of formatting, click **OK**.
7. Select **File | Save As** and keep the same location.
8. Change the **File name** to **Links4**, select **Rich Text Format (*.rtf)** and click **Save**.
9. Select **File | Save as** and keep the same location.
10. Change the **File name** to **Links5** and change **Save as type** to **Web Page (*.htm, *.html)**.
11. Click **Save**.
12. Close any open documents.
13. Minimize *Word* and use the **My Documents** window to view the contents of the folder used to save the files **Links3**, **Links4** and **Links5** above.
14. Double click on **Links3.txt** to open it. If you need to specify an application, choose *Notepad*. The text content is all present, but virtually no formatting and no special features such as images or links have been retained. Close the application.
15. Double click on **Links4.rtf** to open it. If you need to specify an application, choose *Word*. Notice that the content, formatting and features have all been retained.
16. Close the document.
17. Minimize *Word*. Double click on **Links5.htm** to open it. It should open in your default web browser application, e.g. *Microsoft Internet Explorer.* The content is all present, and most of the formatting is retained even though the web page may look a little different.
18. All hyperlinks now work by simple clicking, it is not necessary to hold down the <**Ctrl**> key. Test their operation.
19. Close the browser.
20. Close the window showing the new folder.

Driving Lesson 5 - Revision: Working Efficiently

This is not an ECDL test. Testing may only be carried out through certified ECDL test centres. This covers the features introduced in this section. Try not to refer to the preceding Driving Lessons while completing it.

1. When designing a document, which 2 main factors should be taken into consideration?
2. What types of objects from other software applications can be included in a *Word* document?
3. What is the name for a document that is made up of separate, subdocuments?
4. What feature allows many different documents to be based on the same, consistent look?
5. What feature allows users to move to different locations within a document, or to a different location?
6. Which is the simplest format that a text document can be saved in?
7. Which format allows you to save a document in a format that can be viewed on the Internet?

*See the **Answers** section at the end of the guide.*

If you experienced any difficulty completing this Revision refer back to the Driving Lessons in this section. Then redo the Revision.

Once you are confident with the features, complete the Record of Achievement Matrix referring to the section at the end of the guide. Only when competent move on to the next Section.

Section 2
Text Editing

By the end of this Section you should be able to:

Use Advanced Find and Replace Options

Use Paste Special Options

Use AutoCorrect and AutoFormat

Create AutoText

Change Text Flow and Wrap

To gain an understanding of the above features, work through the **Driving Lessons** in this **Section**.

For each **Driving Lesson**, read the **Park and Read** instructions, without touching the keyboard, then work through the numbered steps of the **Manoeuvres** on the computer. Complete the **Revision Exercise(s)** at the end of the section to test your knowledge.

Driving Lesson 6 - Find and Replace

Park and Read

The **Find and Replace** feature allows you to search a document for specific words, phrases and sentences. However, you can also use it to find or replace other items such as page breaks, paragraph marks and specific formatting of fonts and paragraphs.

Manoeuvres

1. Open the document **Aurora Formatted**, making sure the cursor is at the beginning of the document.

2. Specific formatting in the document can be seen using **Show/Hide**, but in this case, to find the paragraph marks, select **Edit | Find**.

3. Click 

to reveal extra search options.

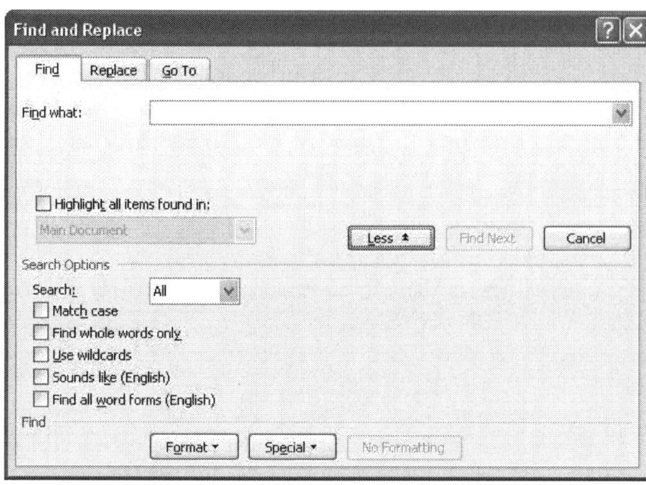

4. Click 

and from the list select **Paragraph Mark**. Notice that **^p** is entered in **Find what**.

5. Click **Find Next** and continue through the document until the following message appears:

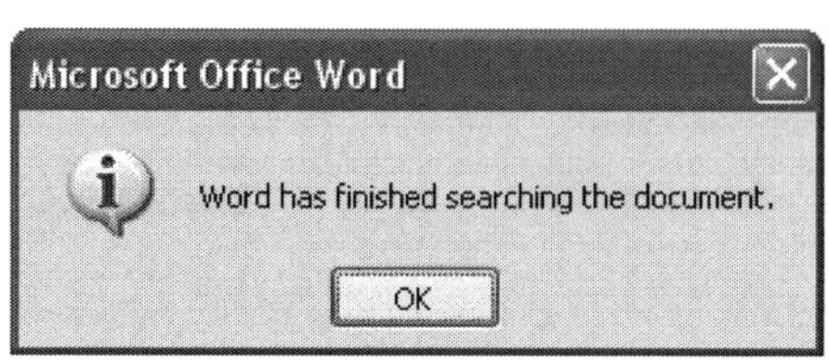

Driving Lesson 6 - Continued

6. Click **OK**.

7. Click Special again and this time find where the manual page break has been made.

8. When you've done this, delete the **^m** entry in **Find what**.

9. To find the paragraph that has been justified, click Format then select **Paragraph**. From **Alignment** select **Justified**.

10. Click **OK** and then **Find Next**. The justified paragraph is highlighted; click **Find Next** again and then **OK** at the message.

11. Click Format and select **Paragraph** again and make sure **Alignment** is cleared. Click **OK**.

12. Click Format and select **Font**. To find the red text in the document click the drop down list for **Font color** and choose red from the grid. Click **OK**.

13. Click **Find Next** to locate the red text. Click **Find Next** again to check for any more red text, then click **OK**.

14. Formatting can also be replaced using the **Replace** feature. Click the **Replace** tab, Place the cursor in the **Replace with** box and click Format and then **Font** and from **Font color,** select **Blue**. Click **OK**.

15. Click **Find Next**. Click **Replace** to change the **red** text to **blue**. Continue to Replace until the **Word has finished...** message appears, click **OK**.

16. To remove the search criteria, place the cursor in the **Find what** box, click Format and then **Font** and from **Font color** select **Automatic**. Click **OK**. Repeat for the **Replace with** box.

*Formatting criteria can be removed quickly from the **Find what** and **Replace with** boxes by clicking the **No Formatting** button with the cursor in the required box.*

17. Special characters can also be replaced using the **Replace** feature. Click the **Replace** tab.

18. With the cursor in the **Find what** box, click **Special** and select **Manual Page Break**.

19. Click in the **Replace with** box, click **Special** and select **Paragraph Mark**.

20. Click **Find Next**. Click **Replace** to change the page break with a paragraph mark.

*A multiple replace is achieved by clicking **Replace All**.*

21. Click **OK** and close the **Find and Replace** dialog box.

22. Close the document <u>without</u> saving.

Driving Lesson 7 - Paste Special Options

Park and Read

Cut and paste is a very useful, time saving feature, but if you simply paste, the text will be added with its original formatting and any styles it contains will automatically be brought into the destination document. **Paste special** gives you more control over how the cut or copied text is added to the document. You can choose whether to paste the text with formatting, or without.

Manoeuvres

1. Start a new, blank document and at the top enter your name. Press <**Enter**>.
2. Open the document **Stylish** and copy paragraphs 1 and 2 (**Background** and **The House**).
3. Switch back to the new document and click **Paste**.
4. Notice how all the styles have been copied with the text from **Stylish** and pasted into your document. This has created a new page, as the style applied to **Background** has a page break before it.
5. Undo the paste action and select **Edit | Paste Special**.

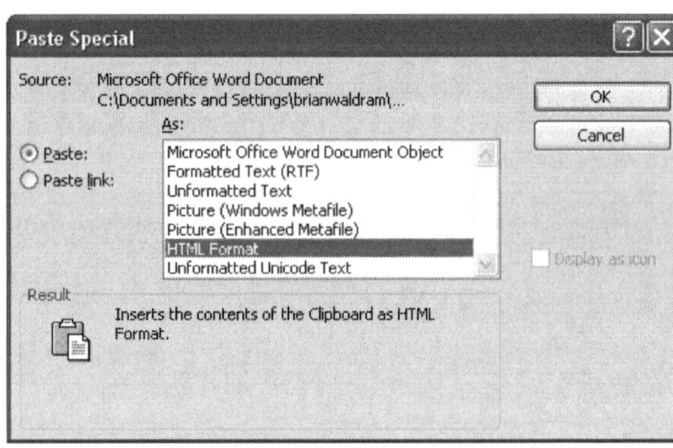

6. Select **Unformatted Text** and click **OK**. Notice how the default formatting of the new document has been applied.
7. Press <**Enter**> and the select **Edit | Paste Special** again. This time select **Formatted Text (RTF)** and click **OK**. All the styles have been brought in again.
8. However, at the end of the pasted text, notice the **Paste Options Smart Tag**, . Click on it - even after pasting you can still remove formatting. Select **Match Destination Formatting** and all the original styles are replaced with those from the new document.
9. Close the documents without saving.

Driving Lesson 8 - AutoCorrect

Park and Read

AutoCorrect is a tool that can automatically replace certain text with alternative text as you type. The most widespread use for this is to correct common spelling errors, so that for example "teh" can be added so that it changes automatically to "**the**". It is also possible to replace common grammatical errors, and there are options to correct capitalisation mistakes.

Manoeuvres

1. Start a new document and type in the following text, exactly as it appears below:

   the ship sailled past the pier and into teh open sea.

2. Notice how the errors are automatically corrected. Now type in the days of the week, each followed by a space, but do not capitalise the first letter. This error is also automatically corrected.

3. To see **AutoCorrect's** range, select **Tools | AutoCorrect Options**. Scroll down the list to see the automatic corrections.

4. Entries can also be added to the dictionary. In the **Replace** box, enter your initials and in the **With** box, enter your full name. Click **Add**, then click **OK**.

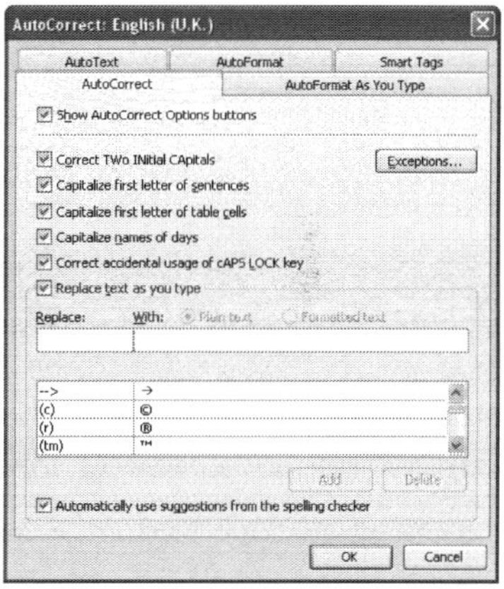

5. Now type in your initials, press <**Spacebar**> and they are automatically replaced with your full name.

6. Select **Tools | AutoCorrect Options**. Scroll through to find your initials in the list.

7. Click on them once to move the entry to the **Replace** and **With** boxes.

8. Change the spelling of your name in the **With** box and click **Replace**. Click **Yes** to redefine the entry. Click **OK**.

9. Now type in your initials in the document, press <**Spacebar**> and they are automatically replaced with your altered name.

10. Select **Tools | AutoCorrect Options**. Scroll through to find your initials in the list.

11. Click on the record and then click **Delete** to remove this entry. Click **OK**.

12. Close the document <u>without</u> saving.

Driving Lesson 9 - AutoFormat

Park and Read

Some formatting of documents can be applied automatically, either as text is being entered or afterwards in a separate step. This is called **AutoFormat**. Once a document has been altered in this way, it is still possible to change the formatting.

Manoeuvres

1. Open the document **Papillon**.
2. Above the first paragraph, enter the title **Background** and press <**Enter**> to create a paragraph title.
3. In the same way, add the title **Escape** to the second paragraph and press <**Enter**>.
4. Make sure there is a blank line between the first paragraph and the title **Escape**.
5. Select **Format | AutoFormat** to display the **AutoFormat** dialog box.

6. Select **AutoFormat now** and click **OK**. Notice how the document has changed.
7. Print the document and close it without saving.
8. Open the document **Aurora**.
9. Add the following paragraph titles, pressing <**Enter**> after each one and making sure that each title is separated from the previous paragraph by a blank line: **Causes**, **Locations**, **Height** and **Mythology**.
10. **AutoFormat** this document.
11. Print it and close it without saving.

Driving Lesson 10 - AutoText

Park and Read

Phrases (or graphics) that are used frequently can be stored in an **AutoText** list, so that they can quickly be added to a document. The required text can be given a different name to identify it and can be called up at any time.

Once an **AutoText** entry has been created, it can be inserted into any document. Some **AutoText** entries already exist within *Word* and can be found within the **AutoCorrect** dialog box.

Manoeuvres

1. Open the document **Apology**.
2. Move to the end of the document and select the text **Customer Care Manager**.
3. Select **Insert | AutoText | New**. The **Create AutoText** dialog box appears.

4. For the **Name** of the **AutoText entry**, type in **Title**. Click **OK**.
5. If there is already an entry with this name, the following dialog box appears.

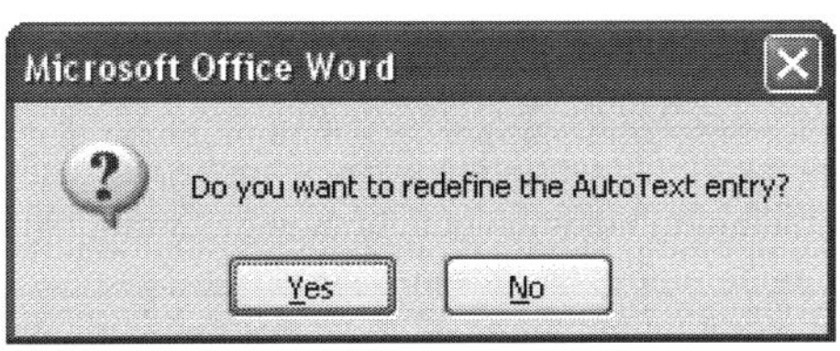

6. To modify any existing entry, select **Yes**.
7. After **at your convenience** in the second paragraph, type **The also wishes to visit you.**.
8. Position the cursor between **The** and **also**, then select **Insert | AutoText | AutoText**.

Driving Lesson 10 - Continued

9. For the **AutoText** to be completed (see step 13) make sure that the **Show AutoComplete suggestions** box is checked.

10. **Title**, the entry created earlier, is available from the list in the **AutoText** dialog box. Scroll down and select it.

11. Click **Insert** to place the **AutoText** in the document.

12. Adjust the spacing if necessary.

13. This process takes too long, there is a better way to use **AutoText**. Move to the end of the document and press <**Enter**> and start to type **Title** and watch for a box to appear.

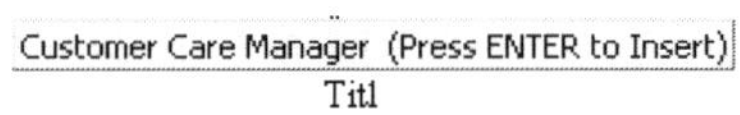

14. Press <**Enter**> to complete the entry.

15. To delete the **Title AutoText**, select **Tools | AutoCorrect Options** and the **AutoText** tab.

16. Scroll down the list and select the **Title** entry.

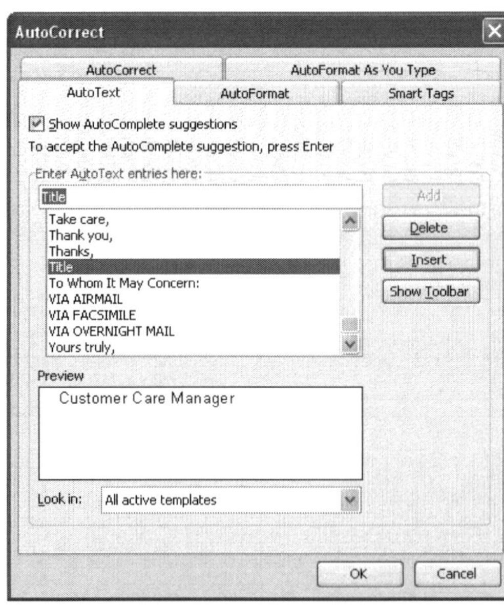

17. Click **Delete** and then **OK**.

18. Close **Apology** <u>without</u> saving and start a new document.

19. Some words, such as days of the week and months, can be inserted automatically. Start to type **Monday** and when the box appears, press <**Enter**> to complete the entry. This is called **AutoComplete**.

20. Select **Insert | AutoText | Closing**.

21. Select **Sincerely yours** from the list.

22. Review the other possible entries from the **Insert | AutoText** menu and insert a selection into the document.

23. Close the document <u>without</u> saving.

Driving Lesson 11 - Text Flow and Wrap

Park and Read

There are a variety of formatting options available when including objects such as graphical objects and tables in text. They can have their own space within the text or they can be included within text blocks so that the text 'wraps' around them. This can be either on one side of the object or the other, or on both sides. Alternatively the object can be placed behind the text.

Manoeuvres

1. Open the **Wrapping** document.
2. Look at the first image on page 2. This is a **Clip Art** image. It has its own fixed space in the text (this example is in its own paragraph) and the layout is known as **In line with text**. This is the default layout when inserting images.
3. Right click on the image and select **Format Picture**. Select the **Layout** tab. The **Wrapping style** is **In line with text**.

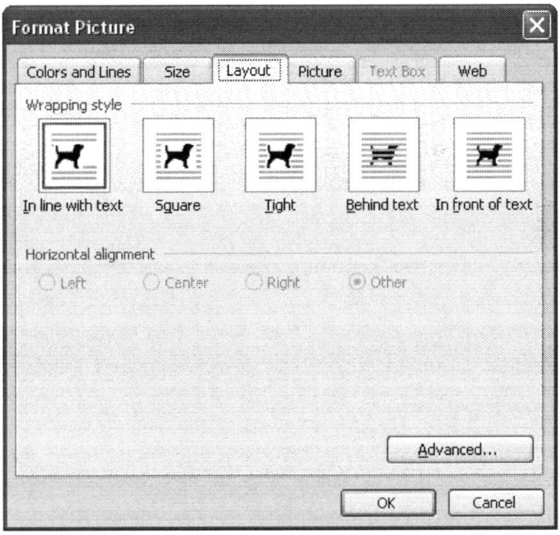

4. Click on the **Square** option for **Wrapping style** and from **Horizontal alignment** select **Right**. Click **OK**. The image is now aligned with the right margin and the text is wrapped on the left.
5. The image is now 'floating'. Drag the image up until it aligns with the top of the first paragraph on the page. As the image is moved, the text is automatically reformatted around it.

Driving Lesson 11 - Continued

6. Right click on the picture of the tower on this page, and select **Format Picture**, **Layout** tab.

7. Select **Square** option for **Wrapping style** and **Left** for **Horizontal alignment**. Click **OK**.

8. Drag the picture to align with the top of the last paragraph on the page.

9. Right click on the picture below the **Pets Corner** text, and select **Format Picture**, **Layout** tab. Select **Tight** option for **Wrapping style** and **Center** for **Horizontal alignment**. Click **OK**.

10. Now the text is wrapped more tightly to the shape of the picture. Drag the picture up until it aligns with the top of the text paragraph.

11. Right click on the **Smiley Face** drawn shape below the **Gift Shop** text, and select **Format Autoshape**, **Layout** tab.

12. Select **Behind text** option for **Wrapping style** and **Center** for **Horizontal alignment**. Click **OK**.

13. The image is now seen behind the text. Drag it up so that it is behind the **Gift Shop** text.

14. Text can be wrapped around other objects. Click in the table in the **Tea Room** text and select **Table | Table Properties | Table** tab.

15. Select an **Alignment** of **Right** and a **Text wrapping** of **Around**.

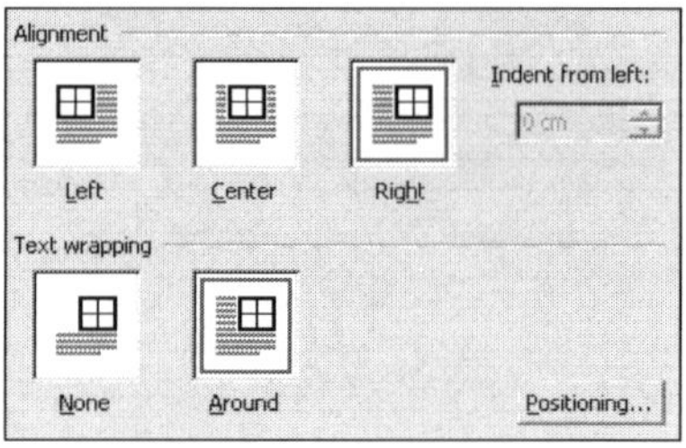

16. Click **OK**.

17. Right click on the **Visitor** chart on the last page and select **Format Object**, **Layout** tab. Select **Square** option for **Wrapping style** and **Right** for **Horizontal alignment**. Click **OK**.

18. Drag the chart up until it aligns with the top of the text paragraph.

19. Right click on the organisation chart on the last page and select **Format Organisation Chart**, **Layout** tab. Select **Square** option for **Wrapping style** and **Left** for **Horizontal alignment**. Click **OK**.

20. Align the chart with the top of the last paragraph.

21. Close the document <u>without</u> saving.

Driving Lesson 12 - Revision: Text Editing

This is not an ECDL test. Testing may only be carried out through certified ECDL test centres. This covers the features introduced in this section. Try not to refer to the preceding Driving Lessons while completing it.

1. Open the document **Birds**.
2. Use the advanced **Find and Replace** options to find **Footnote Marks (Special)**.

Make sure the dialog box does not already contain any formatting search criteria, e.g. font colour red, or this will not work.

3. Find all paragraph marks in the document.
4. On a blank line below the first paragraph, insert the image **branch** from the supplied data.
5. By changing the properties of the picture and moving it, position it so that it appears on the right of the page, aligned with the top of the first paragraph and with the text wrapped around it.
6. Select the picture at the end of the document and change the format so that it appears in the centre of the last paragraph, behind the text.
7. Which method of pasting would you use if you wanted to keep all formatting from the source document?
8. Create an **AutoText** entry, for the text **Created for you by *Your name***.
9. Insert the **AutoText** just created, on a new line at the end of the document.
10. Print the document then delete the **AutoText** entry.
11. Close the document without saving.

*See the **Answers** section at the end of the guide.*

If you experienced any difficulty completing this Revision refer back to the Driving Lessons in this section. Then redo the Revision.

Once you are confident with the features, complete the Record of Achievement Matrix referring to the section at the end of the guide. Only when competent move on to the next Section.

Section 3
Paragraph Editing

By the end of this Section you should be able to:

Amend Line Spacing

Change Paragraph Pagination Options

Create and Modify Styles

Apply Outline Levels to Styles

Work with Multilevel Lists

To gain an understanding of the above features, work through the **Driving Lessons** in this **Section**.

For each **Driving Lesson**, read the **Park and Read** instructions, without touching the keyboard, then work through the numbered steps of the **Manoeuvres** on the computer. Complete the **Revision Exercise(s)** at the end of the section to test your knowledge.

Driving Lesson 13 - Line Spacing

Park and Read

The amount of space between lines in paragraphs can be changed using the **Paragraph** dialog box. Increasing line spacing can sometimes make paragraphs easier to read. There are various advanced spacing options:

At least	minimum spacing - can be adjusted by *Word* to accommodate larger font sizes that would otherwise not fit the spacing specified.
Exactly	specific, fixed spacing that *Word* does not adjust - makes all lines evenly spaced regardless of font size.
Multiple/proportional	spacing increased or decreased by a user specified percentage. For example, set to a multiple of 1.2 to increase spacing by 20%, or by a multiple of 0.8 to decrease spacing by 20%.

Manoeuvres

1. Open the document **Birds** and place the cursor in the first paragraph. This spacing is to be increased proportionally.
2. Select **Format | Paragraph | Indents and Spacing** tab and from **Line spacing** select **Multiple**. From **At** enter **1.2**.

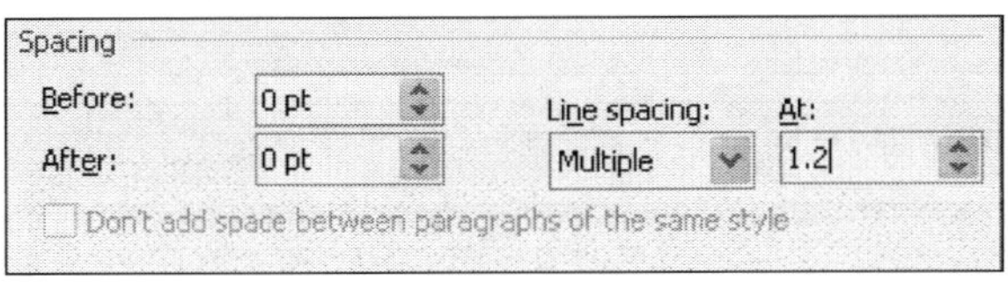

3. Click **OK**.
4. To see what will happen if you reduce this spacing display the **Paragraph** dialog box and type **0.9** in **At**. Click **OK**.
5. Increase the font of this paragraph to **20pt**. Display the dialog box again and from **Line spacing** choose **Exactly** and **12pt**. Click **OK**.
6. Notice that some text has been lost, because the exact spacing is not taking account of the font size.
7. Change the line spacing to **At least 12pt** and notice the difference; *Word* has automatically allowed for the large font.
8. Change the font size back to **10pt**. Change all the paragraph line spacing to **1.5 lines**.
9. Save the document as **Birds2** and close it.

Driving Lesson 14 - Pagination Options

Park and Read

The **Widow/Orphan** control prevents *Word* from separating the last line of a paragraph and printing it at the top of a new page (**widow**), or separating the first line of a new paragraph and leaving it at the bottom of the current page (**orphan**). By default, the control is <u>on</u>.

Manoeuvres

1. Open the document **Widows and orphans**.
2. Scroll down until you can see the bottom of page one and the top of page two on the screen.
3. As the **Widow/Orphan** control is on, two lines of text are kept together at the top of page two.
4. To turn off the control, select the whole document and then **Format | Paragraph** and the **Line and Page Breaks** tab.

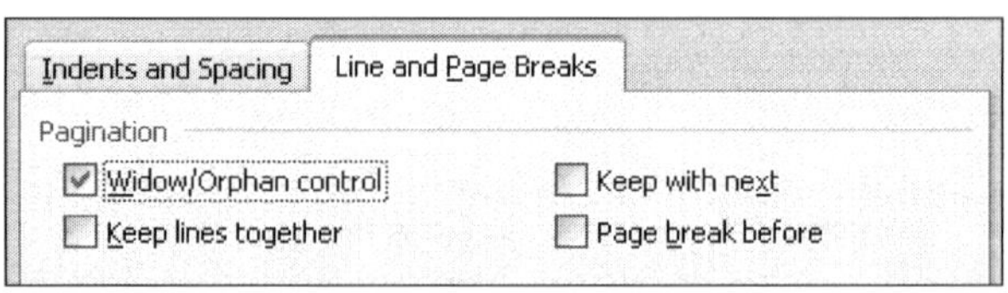

5. From the **Pagination** area, remove the check from the **Widow/Orphan control** box.

*To prevent a paragraph being split over two pages, check the **Keep lines together** option. Use **Keep with next** to prevent a page break between the selected paragraph and the next one. Use **Page break before** to insert a page break before the selected paragraph. To remove any of these options, simply uncheck the relevant box.*

6. Click **OK**.
7. How many lines of text are now left at the top of page two?
8. Turn the control back on by replacing the check in the **Widow/Orphan control** box and click **OK**.
9. Observe how the final line is now joined by the previous one again.
10. Close the document <u>without</u> saving.

*See the **Answers** section at the end of the guide.*

Driving Lesson 15 - Creating Styles

Park and Read

Although there are many formatting styles available by default, it is possible to create others. Styles can be created from scratch or, more usually, they can be based on other styles.

Manoeuvres

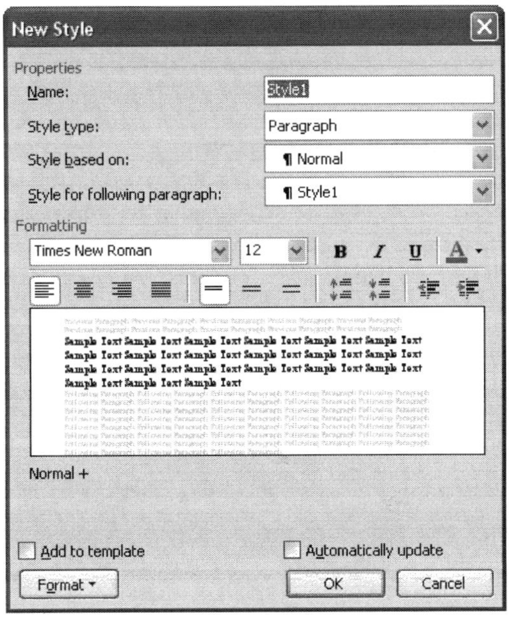

1. Open **Summary** and add the title **Computer Applications**.
2. Select **Format | Styles and Formatting** to display the **Styles and Formatting** task pane.
3. Click on **New Style** to create a new style.
4. In **Name** enter **MainHead**. Make sure **Style based on** shows **Normal** and the **Style type** is **Paragraph**.
5. From the **Formatting** area click on the **Font** drop down list and set the **Font** to **Arial** (or similar).
6. in the dialog box, click the **Bold** button, , the **Center** button,  and change the font size to **14**.
7. Click the **Increase Paragraph Spacing** button, 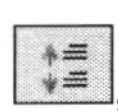, to increase the spacing before and after the style to **6pt**.
8. Click **OK** to finish creating the style.
9. Still within the **Styles and Formatting** task pane, click on **New Style** again and name the style **Text**. Base it on **Normal**.

Two styles cannot have the same name. Style names can be up to 253 characters long but cannot include \, { } or ;.

10. Set the **Font** to **Times New Roman**, **12pt**.

Driving Lesson 15 - Continued

11. Set the **Alignment** to **Justified** and click on **Increase Indent**, , to set the left indent at **1.27cm**. Click **OK** to complete creating the style.

*To customise any of these measurements or settings, click the **Format** button and select an option from the list.*

12. Place the cursor in the title text **Computer Applications**. Click on the drop down arrow from the **Style** box, Normal, on the **Standard** toolbar.

13. Select **MainHead** to format the text accordingly.

14. Add the following headings to the paragraphs:

    Paragraph 1 - Databases
    Paragraph 2 - Word Processing
    Paragraph 3 - Spreadsheets
    Paragraph 4 - Presentations

15. Position the cursor within the first paragraph and choose the **Text** style. Repeat for the remaining paragraphs.

*To create a style using formatted text, select the text, then type the name of the style into the **Style** box on the **Formatting** toolbar,* Normal*. Press <**Enter**>.*

16. Highlight the title **Databases**. Use the **Formatting** toolbar to format the text as **Arial**, **Bold**, **Italic**, **12 pt**.

17. Click on the arrow from the **Style** box and type in **SubHead** to replace the highlighted entry. Press <**Enter**> to create the style based on the selected text.

18. Format the remaining paragraph headings as **SubHead** using the **Style** box drop down list.

19. Create a final new style. This time from **Style type** choose **Character**. Call the style **Highlight**.

20. Select the bold format and the font colour red and click **OK**. Apply the **Highlight** style to the first letter in each word of **Driving Vehicle Licensing Authority**, in brackets in the first paragraph.

21. Save the document as **Applications** and leave it open for the next Driving Lesson.

Driving Lesson 16 - Modifying Styles

Park and Read

Once styles have been created and applied they can be changed at any time. A change to a style will change all the text in a document to which that style has been applied, ensuring continuity throughout the document.

Manoeuvres

1. With **Applications** still open from the previous exercise, select to show **All styles** in the **Styles and Formatting** task pane.
2. Scroll down the **Styles** list and click on the arrow at the right of the **SubHead** style.
3. Click on **Modify** to change the formatting of this style.
4. From the **Modify Style** dialog box, select **Format** then **Font**. Change the **Font** style to **Italic** and check **Small caps** from the **Effects** area.

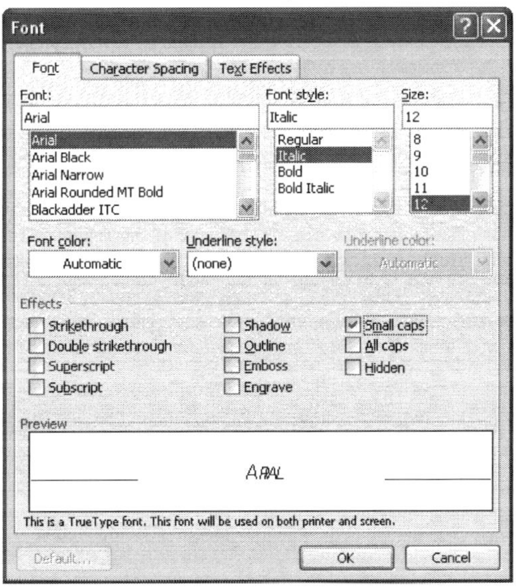

5. Click **OK**. Select **Format | Numbering**, then the **Numbered** tab and choose the second numbering option. Click **OK** then **OK** again.
6. Notice that the text formatted as **SubHead** has now been updated with the changes.
7. Modify the **Highlight** style - change the colour to green and notice the characters formatted with this style have been updated.
8. Save the document and close it.

Driving Lesson 17 - Outline Level Styles

Park and Read

You can assign an **Outline level** paragraph property to styles and then use **Outline View** to show the hierarchy of those styles within a document. By default the styles **Heading 1**, **Heading 2**, have outline levels **1** and **2** respectively, but levels can be assigned to any style.

Within **Outline View**, a document can be collapsed to show only those headings contained within it, or expanded so the entire document can be seen. This view also makes moving around a large document or moving text easier.

Outline level text can be demoted (moved down a level) or promoted (moved up by a level). All of the selected text will then be reformatted accordingly. It is easy to reposition text within a document using **Outline View**. If text formatted as a heading is moved, all text associated with that heading is also moved.

Manoeuvres

1. Open **Stylish**. The heading styles are to have outline levels applied, so that the document can be manipulated in **Outline View**.
2. Modify the **TitleHead**, **MainHead** and **Parahead** styles as follows: select each, in turn, from the **Styles** list in the **Styles and Formatting Task Pane**, then click the arrow at the right of the style name, then **Modify**.
3. Select **Format | Paragraph | Indents & Spacing | Outline level** and apply level **1** to **TitleHead**, level **2** to **MainHead** and level **3** to **Parahead**.
4. Click the **Outline View** button, at the bottom left corner of the screen.
5. The **Outlining** toolbar appears. Use **ToolTips** to find out the functions of the buttons.
6. Click the drop down list as in the diagram below.
7. Select **Show Level 1** on the **Outlining** toolbar. Only the **Title** will be in view.

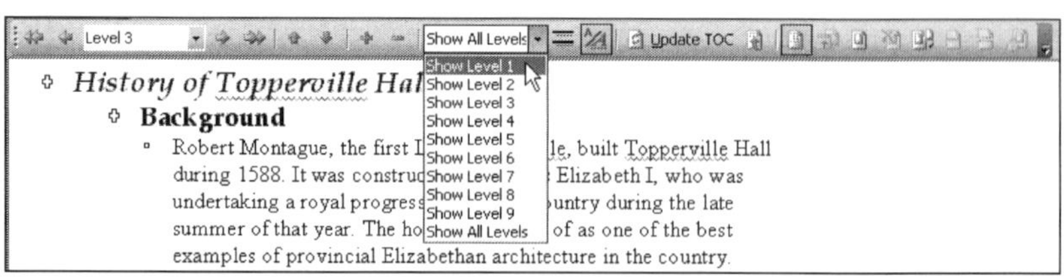

8. Now select **Show Level 2** and notice the change.

Driving Lesson 17 - Continued

9. Select **Show Level 3** to view all of the **ParaHead** titles.
10. Double click on ✥ next to **The Gardens**. This will expand that title only.
11. Double click again to collapse the text.
12. Save the changes to the document and close it.
13. Open the document **Styles** and change to **Outline** view.
14. To move the heading **Equality**, first select the heading and paragraph associated with it.
15. Collapse the text by clicking , from the **Outlining** toolbar.
16. To move the heading and its associated text upwards, position the cursor within the heading and click on **Move Up**, , until the text is above **Background**.
17. To make sure the associated text has been moved, double click to expand the heading.

Text can also be moved by positioning the mouse over the ✥ next to the required text and dragging it to the new position. Double clicking here also expands and collapses text.

18. Collapse the heading again and click on **Move Down**, , to move it back to its original position between **Background** and **Security**.
19. The **Promote** button, , is used to move the text up a style. The **Demote** button, , is used to move the text down a style.
20. Select the main title **E-Commerce**, which is **Heading 1** and click **Demote**, , to change it to **Heading 2**.
21. Collapse all of the remaining paragraphs. Select each of the subheadings in turn (**Heading 2**) and **Demote** them to **Heading 3**.
22. Check what has happened in **Print Layout** view. Switch to **Outline View** and demote the subheadings to **Heading 4**.
23. Now **Promote** the subheadings to **Heading 1** using either the **Promote** button, , or the **Promote to Heading 1** button, .
24. Experiment. Try promoting and demoting different headings.
25. Close the document <u>without</u> saving the changes.

Driving Lesson 18 - Multilevel Lists

Park and Read

Styles for bulleted or numbered lists can be created to contain up to nine levels. A different format can be assigned to each level.

Manoeuvres

1. Start a new document and create a new paragraph style named **Multilist**.
2. Click Format and select **Numbering**.
3. Select the **Outline Numbered** tab and the bullet style, as multi-level bullets, rather than numbers are to be created.

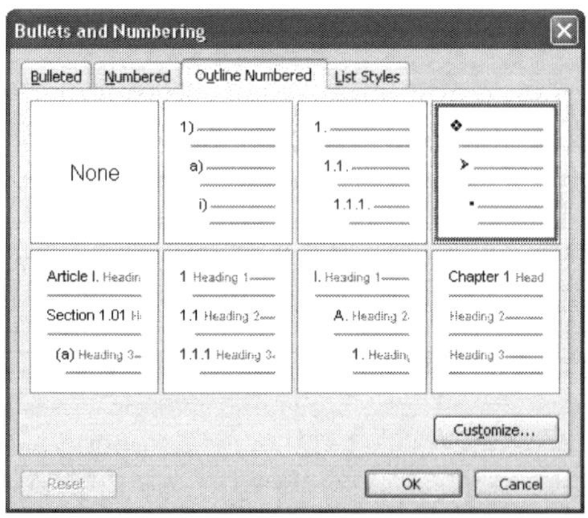

4. Click Customize... to display the **Customize Outline Numbered List** dialog box.

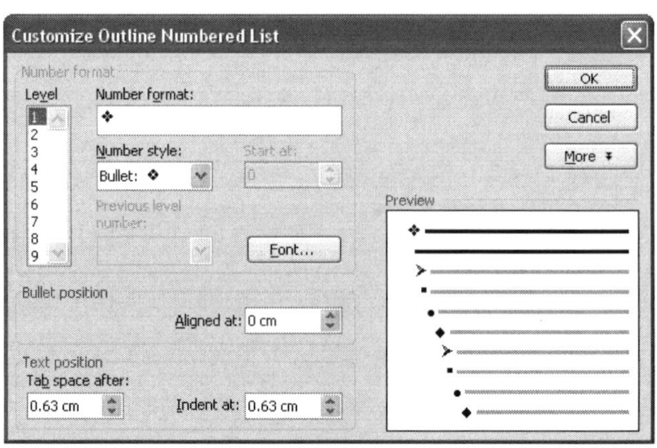

Driving Lesson 18 - Continued

5. This dialog box allows nine different bullet levels to be set, but only three are required here. The **Level 1** bullet is OK. Click on **2** from **Level** and click 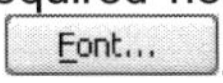

.

6. In the **Font** dialog box, change the **Font color** to **Red** and click **OK**.

7. Leave **Level 3** as it is and click **OK**. Click **OK** again.

8. Type **First**, press <**Enter**>, **Second** <**Enter**>, **Third** <**Enter**>.

9. Click and drag to select the list and from the **Style** drop down list select **Multilist** to apply the new style.

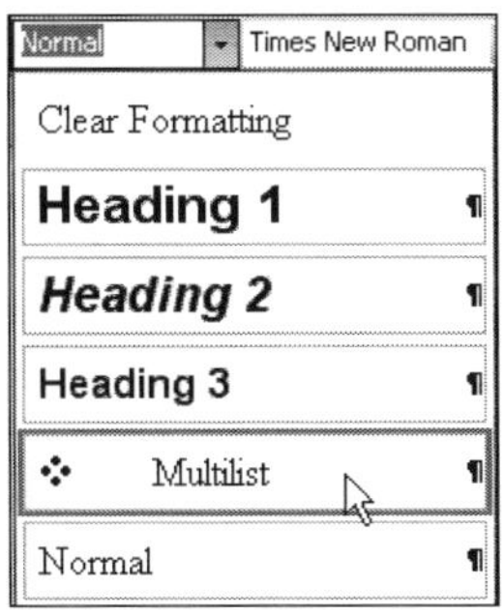

10. The levels are not apparent at the moment. Click in front of **Second** and press <**Tab**>.

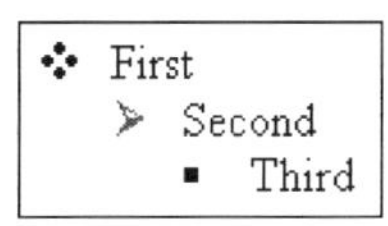

11. Click in front of **Third** and press <**Tab**> twice.

12. Click on the page, away from the list. A multi-level number style is to be created.

13. Create a new style **Multinumbers**.

14. Select **Format | Numbering** and the **Outline Numbered** tab.

15. Select an offset number style that does not contain the word **Heading**, e.g. 1., 1.1., 1.1.1. and click 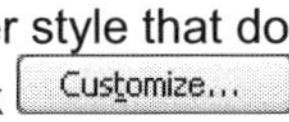

.

16. Leave **Level 1** as it is, but change the font for **Level 2** to **Lucida Handwriting**, click **OK** and change **Level 3** to **Bradley Hand ITC** (choose alternative fonts if these are unavailable). Click **OK**.

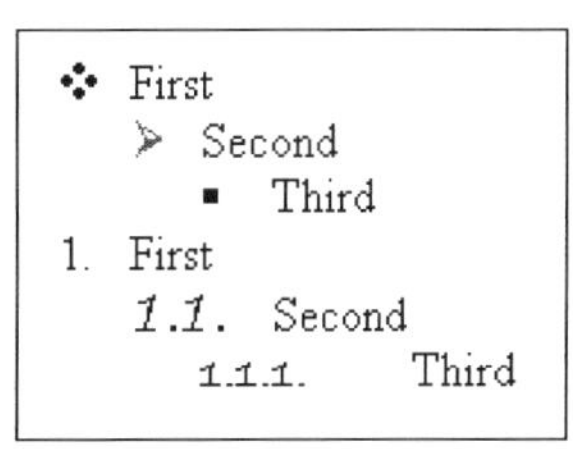

17. Click **OK** twice to return to the document.

18. Create a list as for the bullets and apply the **Multinumbers** style.

19. Use <**Tab**> to create the three levels.

20. Close the document <u>without</u> saving.

Driving Lesson 19 - Revision: Paragraph Editing

This is not an ECDL test. Testing may only be carried out through certified ECDL test centres. This covers the features introduced in this section. Try not to refer to the preceding Driving Lessons while completing it.

1. Open the document **Stately Home**.
2. Change the **Style** of the main heading to **Heading1** and the subheadings to **Heading 3**.
3. Create a new style (**Body**) for the body text, based on **Normal**, with the font as **Tahoma 11pt** and justified with line spacing of **1.5 lines**.
4. Apply the **Body** style to all body text.
5. In **Outline View**, promote all the subheadings to **Heading 2**.
6. Apply a paragraph setting to paragraph 1 of **The Gardens**, so that it will always be kept with the next paragraph.
7. Apply a paragraph setting to the **Pets' Corner** heading so that a new page will be created before it.
8. Save the document as **Stately Home2** and close it.

If you experienced any difficulty completing this Revision refer back to the Driving Lessons in this section. Then redo the Revision.

Once you are confident with the features, complete the Record of Achievement Matrix referring to the section at the end of the guide. Only when competent move on to the next Section.

Section 4
Document Setup

By the end of this Section you should be able to:

Add and Delete Section Breaks

Apply Section Formatting

Apply Headers and Footers to Sections

Create Multiple Columns in a Document

Modify Column Layout, Width and Spacing

Create Watermarks

To gain an understanding of the above features, work through the **Driving Lessons** in this **Section**.

For each **Driving Lesson**, read the **Park and Read** instructions, without touching the keyboard, then work through the numbered steps of the **Manoeuvres** on the computer. Complete the **Revision Exercise(s)** at the end of the section to test your knowledge.

Driving Lesson 20 - Adding/Deleting Section Breaks

Park and Read

When certain pages or parts of a document are to be formatted differently from the rest, e.g. page layout or page numbering, sections are created. Each section can have its own page layout and headers and footers (see later Driving Lesson). A document can have as many sections as required.

Manoeuvres

1. Open the document **Stately Home**. Make sure **Normal** view is selected so you can see the breaks on screen.
2. Position the cursor in front of **The Gardens**.
3. Select **Insert | Break**. From **Section break types**, choose **Continuous**, i.e. it will not start a new page and click **OK**.

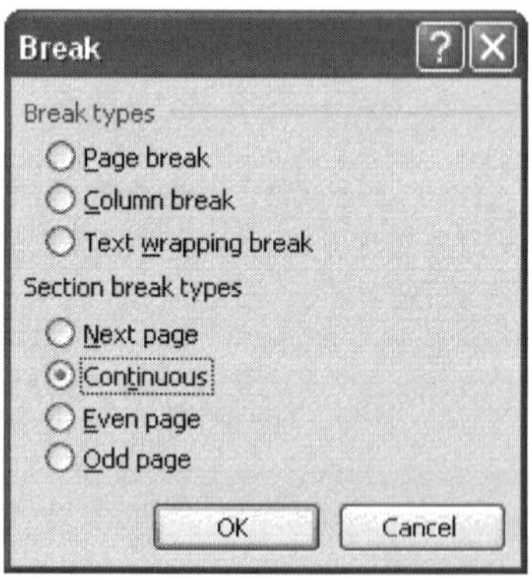

***Even page** and **Odd page Section breaks** will insert a break and start the next section on the next odd or even numbered page of a document.*

4. Insert a **Next page** section break in front of **Pets' Corner**.
5. Section breaks can be changed. The first section break should have been a **Next page** break. To change it, click in the **Gardens** paragraph and select **File | Page Setup**.
6. Select the **Layout** tab and click the **Section Start:** drop down arrow.
7. Select **New page** and click **OK**. The break is changed and the **Gardens** section is now on a separate page.
8. Click in the **Gardens** paragraph and select **File | Page Setup**.
9. Select the **Margins** tab and choose **Landscape** from **Orientation**. Note that **Apply to** shows **This section**. Click **OK**.
10. Scroll through the document to see the pages of the **Gardens** section only are now in landscape.
11. Click in each section break in turn and press <**Delete**>. The breaks are removed and the document reverts to its original appearance.
12. Close the document <u>without</u> saving, so that recent changes are lost.

Driving Lesson 21 - Applying Section Formatting

Park and Read

Once sections have been created in a document, each one can be formatted in a different way. For example, the page layout of one section could be in portrait and another in landscape. Other settings like margins, vertical alignment, headers and footers and columns can also be modified from section to section (columns and headers and footers are described in later exercises).

Manoeuvres

1. Open the document **Stately Home**.
2. Insert continuous section breaks before the following paragraphs: **The House**, **The Gardens**, **Pets' Corner** and **Gift Shop**.
3. With the cursor in the **Pets' Corner** paragraph, select **File | Page Setup | Margins** and set the **Left** and **Right Margins** to **5** cm.
4. Make sure **Apply to** shows **This section** and click **OK**. The new margins are applied to the section. This emphasises this section.
5. Click anywhere in the **House** section and select **File | Page Setup | Layout**.
6. Click the **Section start:** drop down arrow and select **New page**.

7. Click **OK**. The break at the start of the **House** section is changed.
8. Click in the **Gardens** section and repeat the process to change the section break at the end of the **House** section to a **New page** break. The **House** section is now on a separate page.
9. Click anywhere in the **House** section, select **File | Page Setup | Layout**.
10. Click the **Vertical alignment** drop down arrow and select **Center**.

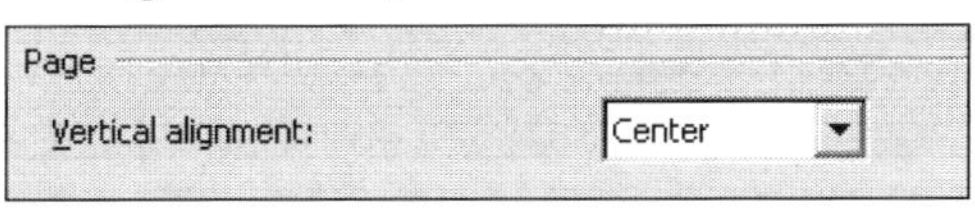

11. Click **OK** and the section is positioned in the centre of the page.
12. Preview the document to show the changes to page **2** and page **4**.
13. Close the document without saving.

Driving Lesson 22 - Section Headers and Footers

Park and Read

Each section in a document can have different headers and footers. This guide has a different header for each section. Headers and footers can be omitted from the first page of a document if desired and different ones can be applied to odd and even pages.

Manoeuvres

1. Open the document **Headers**. This file consists of a front page and four chapters, to which individual headers and footers are to be applied (ignore the repeated text - this is for demonstration only).
2. Insert continuous section breaks on: page **1** after **...stately home**, page **4** end of final paragraph, page **9** end of the paragraph, page **14** end of last paragraph.
3. Go to page **1** and select **File | Page Setup | Layout** tab.
4. In the **Headers and Footers** section on the **Layout** tab, check **Different odd and even** and **Different first page**. There is to be no number on page **1**.

5. Make sure **Apply to** under **Preview** displays **Whole document**, if not use the drop down arrow to select it. Click **OK**.
6. Select **View | Header and Footer**. On page **1** there is only to be a footer with a centred date.
7. Click **Switch Between Header and Footer**, and press <**Tab**> to move to the centre.
8. Click **Insert Date**, to insert the current date then switch to the header.
9. Click **Show Next**, to move to the even page header for section 2 and click **Same as Previous**, to break the automatic link to the first page header.
10. With the cursor at the left of the header, change the font to **Arial** and type **History**. Make the text bold.

Driving Lesson 22 - Continued

11. Switch to the footer and at the left click **Insert Page Number**, . Click  again to remove the link.
12. Switch to the header and move to the header for the odd pages. Break the automatic link.
13. Press <**Tab**> twice to move to the right and type **History**. Format again as **Arial** and make it bold.
14. Switch to the footer and at the right, insert page numbers, making sure the link to the previous section is broken.
15. Continue to create different headers for each section, breaking the link to previous sections as you go.
16. For **Chapter 2** headers, the text **The House** should be at the right on odd pages and at the left on even pages. For the other chapter headers use, **Gardens** and **Pets Corner**.
17. When you have completed all the headers and footers, close the **Header and Footer** view and scroll through the document, checking that page **1** is different from the rest and that all odd and even pages are correct for each chapter.
18. Save the document as **Headers2** and close it.

Driving Lesson 23 - Multiple Column Layout

Park and Read

Columns divide the page vertically. Several columns can be created on a page to create a varied effect. Columns can be applied to the whole document, or to certain parts of it.

Manoeuvres

1. Start a new document and create a **Masthead** (a title that spans the page) with the text **Daily News**.
2. Centre the text and change the font to **Rockwell Extra Bold** (or another bold font if this is not available). Make the text large enough to fill the top line but not so large that it moves on to two lines, e.g. **60pt**.
3. Insert a **Continuous Section** break after the **Masthead** to separate it from the text that is to be inserted.
4. Position the cursor underneath the **Masthead** section break (use ¶ if you can't see the break) and click the **Align Left** button, .
5. Select **Insert | File** and insert the data file **Articles**.
6. With the cursor at the beginning of this text, select **Format | Columns**.
7. Select **Two** from the **Presets** area and make sure the **Apply to** area shows **This section**.

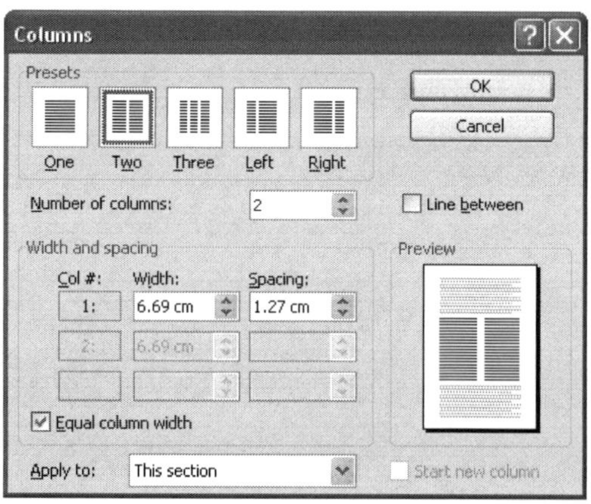

8. Check the **Line between** box to divide the columns with a line and click **OK** to apply the columns (if you are in **Normal View**, *Word* automatically changes to **Print Layout View**).
9. Save the document as **Columns** and leave it open for the next lesson.

Driving Lesson 24 - Modifying Column Layout

Park and Read

Columns can be balanced to divide the text evenly. **Column breaks** are used so that the following text is moved to the top of the next column.

Manoeuvres

1. Use the document **Columns**. Make sure that **Show/Hide** is on so that the column breaks can be seen.
2. Move to the title of the story about the dog.
3. To place this article at the top of the next column, place the insertion point before the **D** of **Dog**.
4. Select **Insert | Break | Column break | OK**. The column break appears as a dotted line across the screen. Notice that the dog article now heads column **2**.

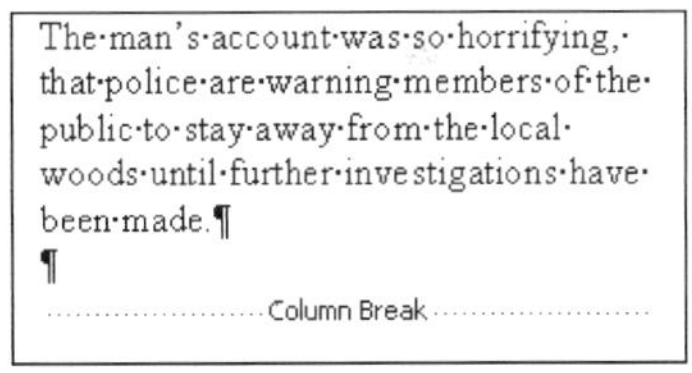

5. Now change the number of columns to **3** and uncheck **Line between** to remove the line between columns. Use a column break to move the **Fundraiser** story to the top of the third column.
6. Print the document.
7. Click on the first column break and press <**Delete**> to remove it.

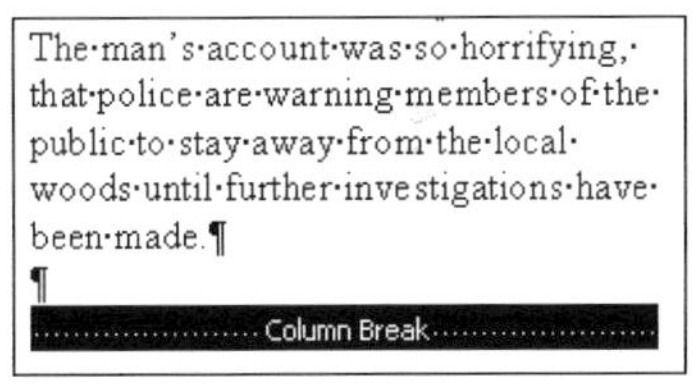

8. Delete the remaining column break to see the changes.
9. Close the document <u>without</u> saving to lose the recent changes.
10. Re-open the document **Columns**.
11. To balance the text in the columns, position the cursor at the end of the text, after the word **proceeds**. Select **Insert | Break | Continuous | OK**.
12. Preview the document. The text should now be equally divided between the two columns.
13. With the cursor in the text, change the number of columns to **3**.
14. Preview the document. The text is still evenly distributed because of the section break.
15. Save the document as **Columns2** and leave it open.

Driving Lesson 25 - Modifying Column Width/Spacing

Park and Read

After columns have been applied to a document, it is possible to change the column width and the spacing between columns.

Manoeuvres

1. Using the document **Columns2**, select **Format | Columns**.
2. Remove the check from the **Equal column width** box in **Width and spacing**.
3. To change the column widths, amend the measurements in the **Width** boxes to something like the following diagram (if these are shown in inches, close the dialog box, select **Tools | Options | General** and select **Centimeters** from the list, then click **OK**).

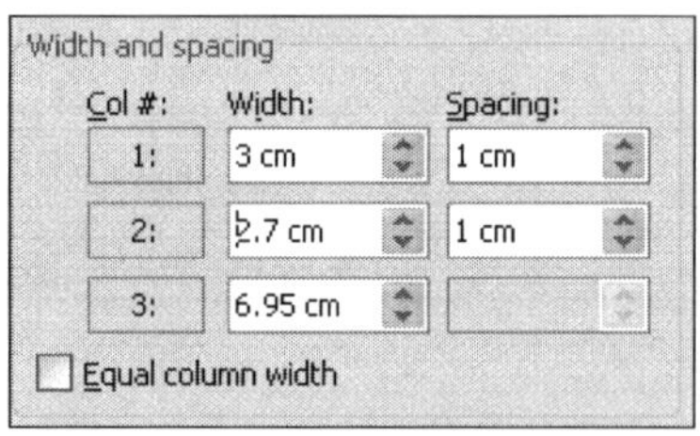

*The **Spacing** will vary depending on your printer's settings.*

4. Notice how the **Preview** changes to show the new column widths.
5. Click **OK** to apply the changes.
6. To change the spacing between the three columns, select **Format | Columns** again.
7. Change the **Spacing** measurements to match the following diagram.

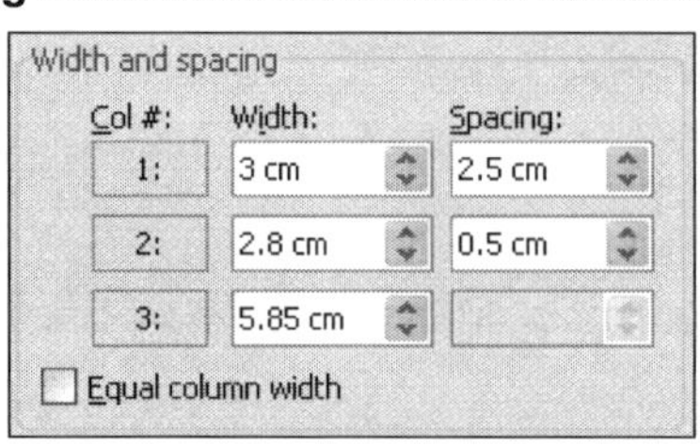

8. Click **OK**.
9. Notice the effect on the document, then close it <u>without</u> saving the changes.

Driving Lesson 26 - Creating a Watermark

Park and Read

A watermark is a piece of text or an image appearing in the background of a document, usually on every page. These can be easily created in *Word*. Watermarks are meant for printed documents only. Watermark text is stored in the Header or Footer of a document.

Manoeuvres

1. Open the document **Wine**.
2. Select **Format | Background | Printed Watermark**. Select **Text watermark** and change the **Text** to **SAMPLE** using the drop down list (text can also be typed into the box).
3. Leave all other settings the same.

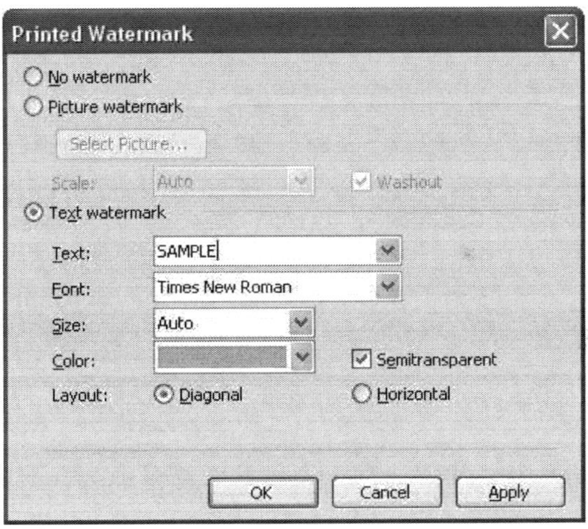

4. Click **OK**.
5. The **Watermark** is added to the header as **WordArt**. Display the **Header** and click on the text **SAMPLE** in the centre of the screen.
6. Close the **Header**.
7. Print the document.
8. Leave the document open for the next Driving Lesson.

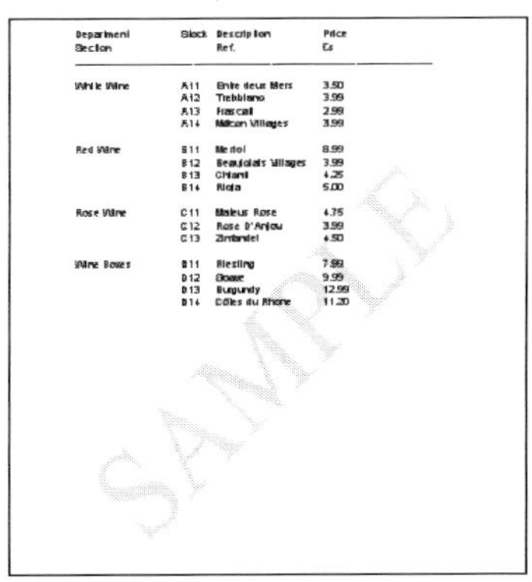

Driving Lesson 27 - Modifying and Deleting Watermarks

Park and Read

After adding a watermark it can be modified by changing the text or by selecting to add a **Picture Watermark** using the **Select Picture** button. **Watermarks** are removed by selecting the **No watermark** option in the **Printed Watermark** dialog box.

Manoeuvres

1. The document **Wine** should still be open. If not, open it.
2. Select **Format | Background | Printed Watermark**.
3. A text watermark is modified by changing the contents of the **Text** box either by entering new text, amending the text already there or by selecting different text from the drop down list. Select the **Text watermark** option, click the drop down list and select **CONFIDENTIAL**. Click **OK**, the watermark has been modified.
4. To insert a picture, select **Format | Background | Printed Watermark**.
5. Select the **Picture watermark** option and then click **Select Picture** and locate the data files from **Look in**. Select the **watermark** file and click **Insert**.
6. In the **Printed Watermark** dialog box, ensure **Washout** is checked so the graphic is not too vivid.
7. Click **OK**. Print a copy of the document.
8. To delete a watermark select **Format | Background | Printed Watermark**. Select the **No watermark** option and click **OK**. All types of watermark can be removed in this way.

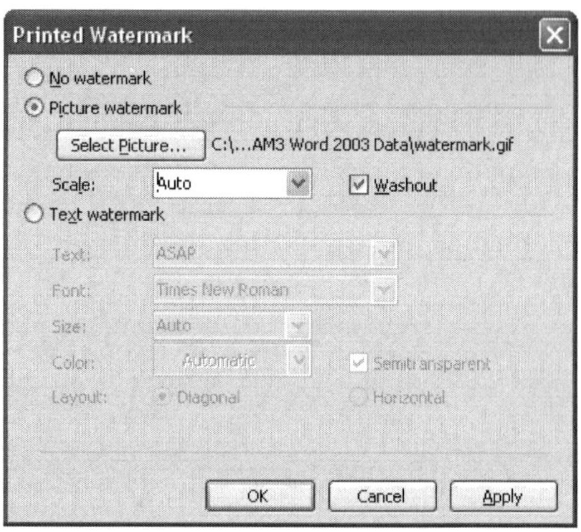

9. Close the document <u>without</u> saving.

Driving Lesson 28 - Revision: Document Setup

This is not an ECDL test. Testing may only be carried out through certified ECDL test centres. This covers the features introduced in this section. Try not to refer to the preceding Driving Lessons while completing it.

1. Open the document **Predators**.
2. Insert **Continuous** section breaks in front of the **Body Form** title and before the **Conclusion**.
3. Insert a **Next page** section break before the **Senses** section.
4. Change the left and right margins to **4 cm** in the **Senses** section only.
5. Apply 2 columns from **Body Form** to **Methods of Reproduction**.
6. Reduce the spacing between the columns to **1cm**.
7. Apply headers and footers of your choice, but make sure that the first page header and those for odd and even pages are different.
8. Apply a text watermark, **DO NOT COPY**, to the document.
9. Print the document.
10. Close it <u>without</u> saving.

If you experienced any difficulty completing this Revision refer back to the Driving Lessons in this section. Then redo the Revision.

Once you are confident with the features, complete the Record of Achievement Matrix referring to the section at the end of the guide. Only when competent move on to the next Section.

Section 5
Tables

By the end of this Section you should be able to:

AutoFormat Tables

Merge and Split Cells

Convert Text to a Table

Sort Data

Perform Calculations

Change Table Properties and Setup

To gain an understanding of the above features, work through the **Driving Lessons** in this **Section**.

For each **Driving Lesson**, read the **Park and Read** instructions, without touching the keyboard, then work through the numbered steps of the **Manoeuvres** on the computer. Complete the **Revision Exercise(s)** at the end of the section to test your knowledge.

Driving Lesson 29 - Table AutoFormat

Park and Read

You can quickly give your table a professional design by using one of *Word*'s built-in table formats. You can also create your own table style.

Manoeuvres

1. Open the document **Staffing**.
2. Place the cursor within the table and select **Table | Table AutoFormat**.

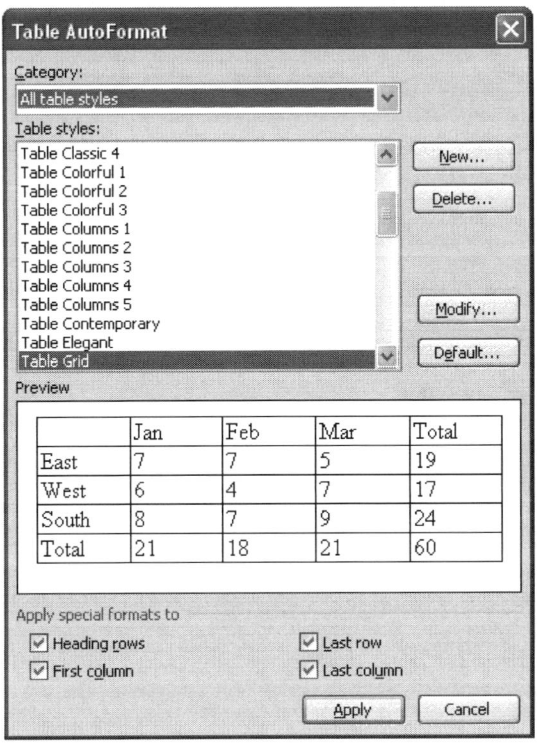

3. Scroll through the list of **Table styles** and select some to see the **Preview** change.
4. Select **Table 3-D effects 2** and click **Apply**.

*To create a new table style, click the **New** button in the **Table AutoFormat** dialog box and choose the required settings. The new style will then appear in the **Table styles** list.*

5. Save the document as **Staffing2** and close it.

Driving Lesson 30 - Merging & Splitting Cells

Park and Read

Cells in a table can be **merged** or **split**. To merge cells means to join two or more cells together to make one large cell. To split cells means to divide a cell into two or more cells.

Manoeuvres

1. In a new document, create a table with **5** columns and **10** rows.
2. Move to the second cell on the top line, select that cell and the cell to the right of it. Select **Table | Merge Cells**. The cells are merged.

*The **Merge Cells** button, , on the **Tables and Borders** toolbar can also be used.*

3. Merge the two cells at the right of the top row then all of the cells on the second row.
4. Merge cells 1 and 2 on rows 3 to 9. This must be done one row at a time.
5. Merge cells 1 to 4 on the bottom row.
6. Your employer wants you to keep a record of daily sales to keep in your Personal Development folder. Enter text into the table until it matches the diagram below.

Date	Name		Department	
Product		Price	Quantity	Total Price
Grand Total				

7. Your employer now decides that product reference numbers should be added to the table. Position the cursor in the cell containing **Product** and select **Table | Split Cells**.

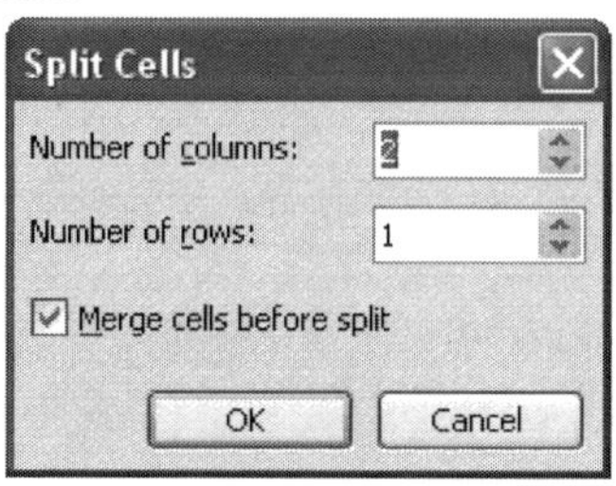

Driving Lesson 30 - Continued

8. Make sure **2 columns** and **1 row** are selected from the **Split Cells** dialog box and click **OK**.

9. Enter **Ref.** in the cell to the right of **Product** and split the cells in the six rows below (use the **Split Cells** button, , on the **Tables and Borders** toolbar).

Date	Name		Department	
Product	Ref.	Price	Quantity	Total Price
Grand Total				

Cells that have not been merged can still be split.

10. Save the document as **Sales Checklist** and close it.

Driving Lesson 31 - Converting Text to a Table

Park and Read

Existing text can be converted to table format, providing the text is already separated into fields. This can be done with commas, tabs or paragraph marks. It may be necessary to remove any extra commas or tabs to reach the required format.

Manoeuvres

1. Open the document **Diary**. Select all of the text.
2. From the menu select **Table | Convert | Text to Table**.

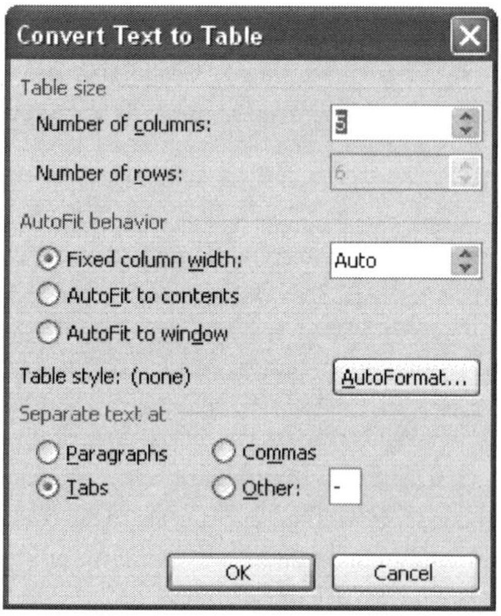

3. The **Number of columns** should be correct. Check that **Separate text at** selection shows **Tabs** and click **OK**.
4. The text will now be in table format. Apply formatting to the table, as desired.
5. Save the document as **Converted** and close it.

*To convert a table into text, select the table and from the menu choose **Table | Convert | Table to Text**. From the **Convert Table to Text** dialog box, choose how the text is to be separated. Click **OK**.*

Driving Lesson 32 - Sorting Table Data

Park and Read

A table can be sorted in order of any column, with secondary sorts being applied, if required. Ascending or descending sorts can be performed on text or numbers.

Manoeuvres

1. Open the document **Vacation**. This shows the holiday entitlement of staff members.

2. Make sure the cursor is within the table. Select **Table | Sort** to display the **Sort** dialog box.

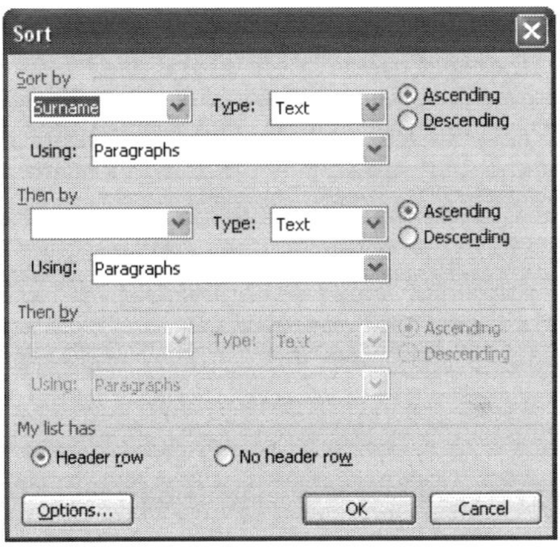

3. Check that **Header row** is checked in the **My list has** area. The **Sort by** choices will now show the column headings.

4. Select **Surname** and **Ascending**. Click **OK** to sort the surnames **A-Z**.

Holiday Chart

Surname	Initial	Department	Days Holiday
Baker	S	Training	3
Borland	J	Administration	0
Chapman	I	Finance	17
Chesterton	I	Training	0
Clarke	A	Advertising	0
Collins	P	Administration	5
Gardner	P	ET Trainee	0
Harvey	D	Transport Pool	1
Leigh	C	Administration	3
Myers	A	Computer Services	0
Phillips	L	Personnel	2
Smith	F	Finance	1
Smith	John	Production	4
Smith	James	Production	2
Waldram	B	Computer Services	2
Waterman	D	Computer Services	7
Westgarth	S	Catering	0
Wright	B	Training	4

Driving Lesson 32 - Continued

5. Now, with the cursor in the table, select **Table | Sort**. Select **Surname** and **Descending**, then click **OK** to sort the surnames **Z-A**.

Holiday Chart

Surname	Initial	Department	Days Holiday
Wright	B	Training	4
Westgarth	S	Catering	0
Waterman	D	Computer Services	7
Waldram	B	Computer Services	2
Smith	F	Finance	1
Smith	John	Production	4
Smith	James	Production	2
Phillips	L	Personnel	2
Myers	A	Computer Services	0
Leigh	C	Administration	3
Harvey	D	Transport Pool	1
Gardner	P	ET Trainee	0
Collins	P	Administration	5
Clarke	A	Advertising	0
Chesterton	I	Training	0
Chapman	I	Finance	17
Borland	J	Administration	0
Baker	S	Training	3

6. Again, with the cursor within the table, select **Table | Sort**. From the **Sort by** selection, choose **Days Holiday**, (note the **Type** changes automatically to **Number**), **Descending** and click **OK**.

Holiday Chart

Surname	Initial	Department	Days Holiday
Chapman	I	Finance	17
Waterman	D	Computer Services	7
Collins	P	Administration	5
Wright	B	Training	4
Smith	John	Production	4
Leigh	C	Administration	3
Baker	S	Training	3
Waldram	B	Computer Services	2
Smith	James	Production	2
Phillips	L	Personnel	2
Smith	F	Finance	1
Harvey	D	Transport Pool	1
Westgarth	S	Catering	0
Myers	A	Computer Services	0
Gardner	P	ET Trainee	0
Clarke	A	Advertising	0
Chesterton	I	Training	0
Borland	J	Administration	0

7. Repeat this sort, adding **Surname**, **Ascending** in the **Then by** section. Select **OK** to sort the list by the amount of holidays, then **A-Z** by surname at the same time.

8. Who is last on the list?

9. Save the document as **Vacation2**, obtain a printed copy and close it.

If lines and borders have already been added to a table, these will be sorted along with the data. It may be prudent to remove all lines and then replace them, if necessary, after sorting.

*See the **Answers** section at the end of the guide.*

Driving Lesson 33 - Performing Calculations

Park and Read

Calculations can be carried out within a table. A column of numbers can be summed, or any basic calculation can be performed on the data within the table. Every formula must start with the equals sign **=**. Standard mathematical functions are used to create formulas.

Like a spreadsheet, each column in a table is referred to by a letter: **A**,**B**,**C**,**D**, etc., whilst rows are referred to by numbers: **1**, **2**, **3**, **4**, etc. The cell address, e.g. **A1**, is the position where the row and column intersect. It is this cell address that will be used to build formulas, e.g. **=A1 + A2**.

Manoeuvres

1. Create a **5 x 5** table in a new document.
2. In the first column (column **A**) enter a list of four numbers.
3. With the cursor in the last cell of the column, select **Table | Formula**. The formula dialog box suggests a formula that may be appropriate.

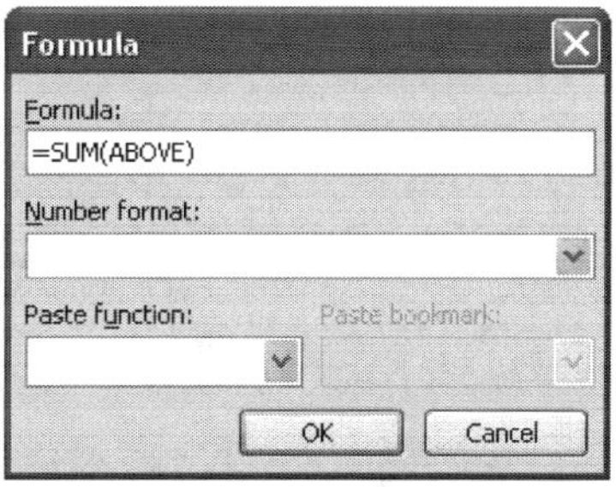

4. In this case the **SUM** field code is required. Use the **Number format** drop down to select **0.00**, click **OK** and the sum is complete with 2 decimal places.
5. With the field code highlighted, select **Table | Formula** and using the **Number format** drop down select **0**, a format with no decimal places. Click **OK** to apply the different number format.
6. Place the cursor in cell **B2**. Select **Table | Formula**. Delete the suggested formula and enter **=a1*a2**. Click **OK**. The answer will be displayed.
7. In cell **B3** use the same method to calculate **a2/a1**.
8. To calculate the **Product** of the above two cells, with the cursor in **B4**, open the **Formula** dialog box and remove the suggested formula. Type **=**. From the drop down list under **Paste function**, select **Product**.
9. In the brackets insert **B2,B3**. The formula should read **=PRODUCT(B2,B3)**, the equivalent of **B2*B3**. Click **OK** to perform the calculation.
10. Close the document without saving.

*If any numbers are changed the formula is not automatically updated. However, while the formula cell is selected, pressing <**F9**> will recalculate it.*

Driving Lesson 34 - Table Properties and Setup

Park and Read

Various aspects of a table can be changed, for example the cell margins, text alignment and direction. If the table is large, you can apply settings so that the heading rows are repeated on each page, or so that rows either break or don't break across pages.

Manoeuvres

1. Open the document **Company** and select the top row of the table - the text direction is to be changed.
2. Select **Format | Text Direction**. From the dialog box select the lower left option.

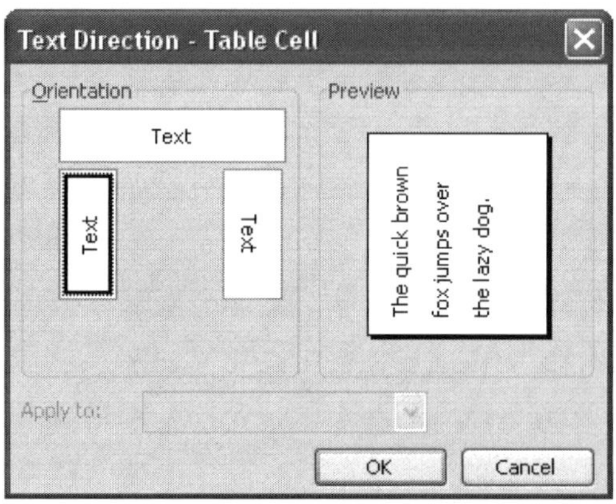

3. Click **OK** to see the headings change.
4. They actually looked better originally; use the same method to correct them.
5. The top row of the table is now too large and the other rows could be wider. Double click on the table select icon, ⊞, at the top left corner and choose the **Row** tab of the **Table Properties** dialog box.
6. Check **Specify height** and enter **0.8 cm** in the box. Ensure **At least** is selected.

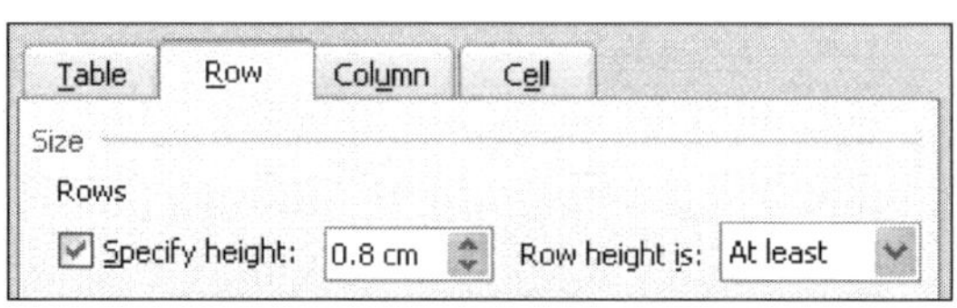

Driving Lesson 34 - Continued

7. Click **OK**. This increases the height of all the rows in the table.
8. Display the table properties again and select the **Cell** tab. Click **Options**.
9. In **Cell Options** remove the check from **Same as the whole table** so that the cell margins can be changed. Change the **Top** cell margin to **0.2 cm** (to move the text down in every cell) and the **Left** cell margin to **0.4 cm** (to move the text further to the right in every cell).

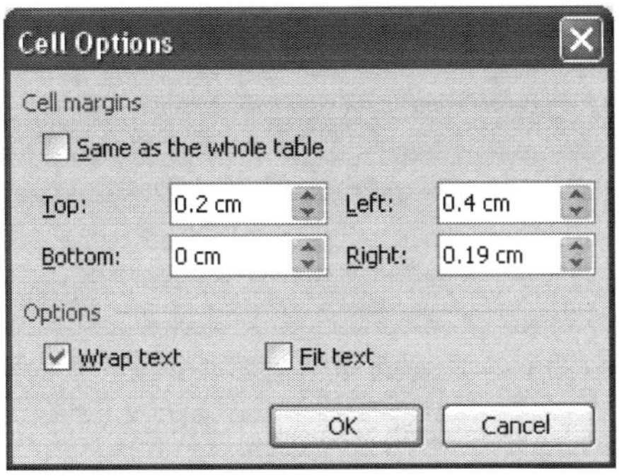

10. Click **OK** twice to see the results. The text in every cell is further from the top and more to the right.
11. With the whole table still selected, display the **Table Properties** dialog box again. From the **Cell** tab, in the **Vertical alignment** section, the available options are **Top**, **Center** and **Bottom**. Select **Bottom** from and click **OK**. The text is moved to the bottom of each cell.

12. Place the cursor in front of the surname on the bottom row on page **1**. Press <**Enter**> until the text moves to the next page. This row has been split across 2 pages.
13. Select the table and display **Table Properties**. On the **Row** tab, notice **Allow row to break across pages** is checked.
14. Clear the check and click **OK**. Notice that all the data from the row is now back together.
15. Remove the 2 paragraph marks added previously, the row moves back to page 1.
16. If a table is split over more than one page it's a good idea to have headings on each page. Select the top row and make it bold. With the top row still highlighted, select **Table | Table Properties** and the **Row** tab.
17. Check **Repeat as header row at the top of each page**. Click **OK**.
18. Check the top of each page to see the header row.
19. Save the document as **Company2** and close it.

Driving Lesson 35 - Revision: Tables

This is not an ECDL test. Testing may only be carried out through certified ECDL test centres. This covers the features introduced in this section. Try not to refer to the preceding Driving Lessons while completing it.

1. Start a new document.
2. Create a new table to match the table below, an invoice (you will need to merge cells).

Invoice				
Ref No	Description	Qty	Price	Total
Subtotal				
VAT				
Total				

3. Print the document and close it <u>without</u> saving.
4. Open the document **Quotas**.
5. Convert the text to a table (separated at tabs).
6. Calculate the total sales for each salesperson.
7. Print the document and close it <u>without</u> saving.
8. Start a new document and create a **4x6** table containing a list of five types of car.
9. The headings should be **Manufacturer**, **Model**, **Colour** and **Price**.
10. Enter a fictional price for each car.
11. Sort the table in ascending alphabetical order by model.
12. Now sort the table numerically by price, from highest to lowest.
13. Sort the table alphabetically by **Colour**.
14. Save the document as **Car sort** and close it.

If you experienced any difficulty completing this Revision refer back to the Driving Lessons in this section. Then redo the Revision.

Once you are confident with the features, complete the Record of Achievement Matrix referring to the section at the end of the guide. Only when competent move on to the next Section.

Section 6
Referencing

By the end of this Section you should be able to:

Create, Modify & Delete Footnotes & Endnotes

Create, Format & Update a Table of Contents

Add & Delete Bookmarks

Create & Delete Cross-references

Add Captions

Create a Table of Figures

Create & Edit Index Entries

To gain an understanding of the above features, work through the **Driving Lessons** in this **Section**.

For each **Driving Lesson**, read the **Park and Read** instructions, without touching the keyboard, then work through the numbered steps of the **Manoeuvres** on the computer. Complete the **Revision Exercise(s)** at the end of the section to test your knowledge.

Driving Lesson 36 - Creating Footnotes and Endnotes

Park and Read

Footnotes are a formalised way of documenting sources for quotations, facts and ideas in a report. A footnote number is automatically placed in the document next to the text to be referenced. The same number appears at the bottom of the page with details about the source of the information. **Endnotes** perform the same function, but are found at the end of a document.

Manoeuvres

1. Open the document **Discovery**.
2. To create a footnote, position the cursor after **tomb** in the first paragraph and select **Insert | Reference | Footnote**.
3. The **Footnote and Endnote** dialog box appears. Make sure that the **Footnotes** option is checked and that **Numbering** shows **Continuous** then click **Insert**.

4. The cursor moves to the bottom of the page, ready for the text to be entered into a special footnote area. Enter the following text: **Evidence was found of early grave robbers**.
5. Use the scroll bar to move back to the main document and notice how the **reference mark**, the number **1**, has been inserted in the correct place.
6. Move the mouse over the reference mark to display the footnote as a caption.

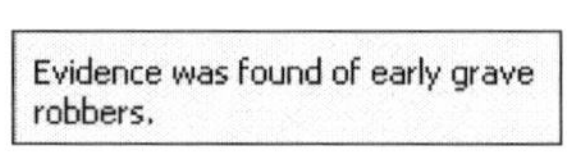

*If using **Normal View** the footnotes can only be seen with **View | Footnotes** switched on.*

Driving Lesson 36 - Continued

7. Insert the following footnotes:

    Paragraph **2**, after **Carter**: **Lord Caernarvon financed the dig.**.

    Paragraph **3**, after **canopic jars**: **Alabaster or clay pots with the heads of Egyptian deities for lids. Each watched over a particular body part.**.

    Paragraph **4**, after **bandaged body**: **Jewels and other precious items were found in the wrappings.**.

8. Save the document as **Noted** and close it.
9. Open **Discovery** again.
10. Insert a page break before the fourth paragraph.
11. Position the cursor after **tomb** in the first paragraph and select **Insert | Reference | Footnote**.
12. This time select to insert an **Endnote** and click **Insert**.
13. Enter the same text as in step **4**.
14. Insert the notes in step **7** as **Endnotes**.
15. Print the document.
16. Endnotes can be converted to footnotes and vice versa. Select **Insert | Reference | Footnote** and click **Convert**.

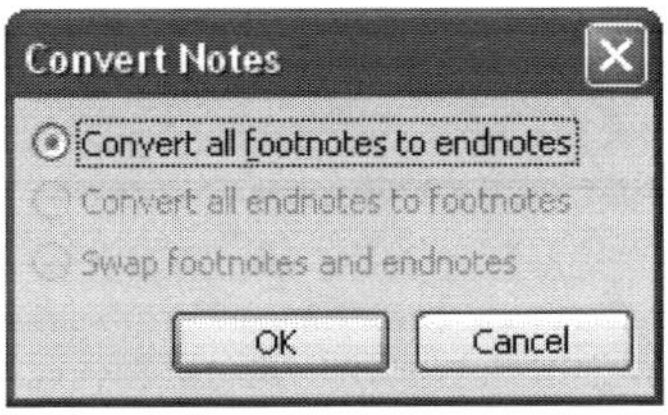

17. Ensure **Convert all endnotes to footnotes** is selected and click **OK**.
18. Click **Close**. Footnotes have replaced the endnotes.
19. To convert them back to endnotes, select **Insert | Reference | Footnote** and click **Convert**.
20. Select **Convert all footnotes to endnotes** and click **OK**, then click **Close**.
21. Save it as **Endnotes** and close it.

*Footnotes (but not captions) are always displayed in **Print Layout** view.*

Driving Lesson 37 - Modifying/Deleting Footnotes and Endnotes

Park and Read

Footnotes and endnotes can be edited, formatted and deleted in the same way as normal text. There is a widely observed convention that footnote reference numbers are entered in superscript form.

Manoeuvres

1. Open the file **Birds**. This document contains four footnotes.
2. The footnotes are displayed at the bottom of the screen and the **Captions** are displayed when the cursor moves over one in the text. Move the cursor to **Footnote 1** and read the caption.
3. There is a mistake in the second footnote, the food referred to is **fat balls** and not **fatballs**. Edit the text as required.

Double click on a reference number in the text to go directly to a footnote or endnote.

4. Select the first reference mark in the text and then delete it. The footnote text is also removed and the remaining footnotes are automatically renumbered.

If a footnote is deleted, the footnote reference mark is not removed. However, if the reference mark is deleted, the corresponding footnote is removed along with it. Great care, therefore, must be exercised when removing footnote reference marks.

5. Use **Print Preview** to check the appearance of the document.
6. Print a copy of the document and close it without saving the changes.

Driving Lesson 38 - Creating a Table of Contents

Park and Read

It is possible in *Word* to create various reference features in a document such as **tables of contents**, **indexes**, **cross references**, and **captions**. Once these tables are created, they can automatically be updated, if any of the information is changed.

A table of contents is based on styles within a document. Certain heading styles are chosen, and all text in the document that uses these styles is automatically included in the contents.

Manoeuvres

1. Open **Topperville Hall**. This document has already been formatted with **Heading** styles.
2. Place the cursor on the blank line below the title, press <**Enter**>, type **Contents** and press <**Enter**> again.
3. Select **Insert | Reference | Index and Tables** and the **Table of Contents** tab.

*If the **Table of Contents** is being created from newly created styles, rather than existing styles, click the **Options** button to specify the order of styles being used. From **Available styles**, remove the level numbers and insert the correct number next to the required style. To check that the table shows the correct styles at the correct level, look at the **Preview** before clicking **OK**.*

4. To see different formats, choose each type in turn from the **Formats** drop down list. The preview shows the effects.
5. Select **Formal**, then click **OK** to create a table of contents.

History of Topperville Hall

Contents

6. Save the document as **Contents** and leave it open.

Driving Lesson 39 - Updating a Table of Contents

Park and Read

Once a table of contents has been created, it is an easy matter to update it if any changes are made to the contents themselves.

Manoeuvres

1. The **Contents** document should still be open. If not, open it.
2. To check that the page numbers are correct, hold down <**Ctrl**> and click on a page number in the table of contents. The cursor moves to the relevant place in the document.
3. Insert a **Page Break** before **Introduction** (<**Ctrl Enter**>). The page numbers in the table of contents are now incorrect.
4. To update the table of contents, place the cursor within it and press <**F9**>.

If difficulty is encountered when positioning the cursor, use the cursor keys.

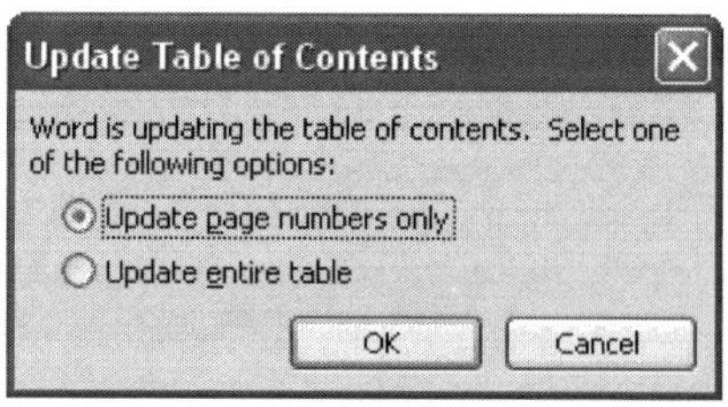

5. When the **Update Table of Contents** dialog box appears, select the **Update page numbers only** option. Click **OK**.
6. Check the page numbers - they should now be correct.

*Tables can be automatically updated prior to printing by setting the **Update Fields** option in **Tools | Options | Print**.*

7. Save the document as **Contents** then close it.

Driving Lesson 40 - Adding and Deleting Bookmarks

Park and Read

A **bookmark** can be assigned to a text position or to a graphic within a document. Once a place within a document has been given a bookmark, there are various methods to locate it quickly and easily. This can be a very useful feature in a large, complex document.

Manoeuvres

1. Open the file **Predators** and position the cursor on page **2**, at the beginning of the **Senses** heading.
2. From the menu select **Insert | Bookmark**.

3. Enter **Senses** as the **Bookmark name**.

A bookmark name cannot contain spaces.

4. Click **Add** to create the bookmark.
5. Create a second, appropriately named bookmark for the **Conclusion** on page **3**.
6. Insert a graphic of a shark from **Clip Art** after the **Diet** paragraph.
7. Select the graphic, then select **Insert | Bookmark**.

Driving Lesson 40 - Continued

8. Enter **sharkpic** as the **Bookmark name** and then click **Add**.
9. Select the first sentence of the **Teeth** paragraph and insert a bookmark named **toothache**.
10. Move the cursor to the beginning of the document.
11. Select **Edit | Go To** to display the **Find and Replace** dialog box.
12. Select **Bookmark** from the **Go to what** box and the **Senses** bookmark from the bookmark name list.

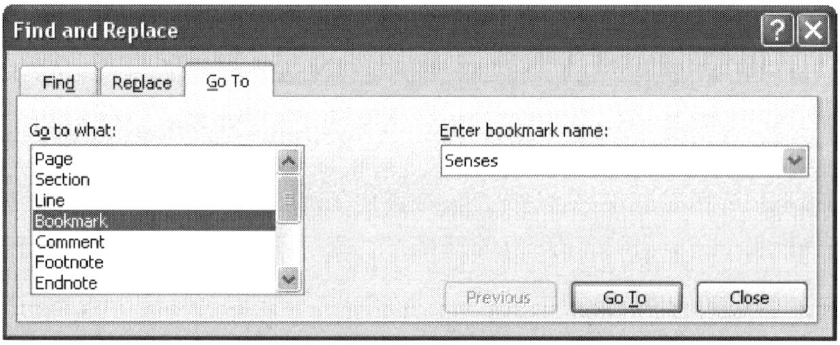

13. Click the **Go To** button to go to the **Senses** section. You may need to move the dialog box to see the result.
14. In the same way, use bookmarks to move to the other bookmarked text and the graphic.
15. Close the **Find and Replace** dialog box.
16. To delete the **Senses** bookmark, select **Insert | Bookmark**.
17. Select the **Senses** bookmark from the list.
18. Click the **Delete** button, then click **Close**.
19. Close the document <u>without</u> saving.

Driving Lesson 41 - Cross-Referencing

Park and Read

Cross-referencing is a method of placing a reference in a document, which refers to an item elsewhere in a document, such as a **heading**, **bookmark**, **caption**, etc. When a cross-reference is created there are a variety of options for the reference text, including page number, heading text, bookmark text, etc. If the cross reference is defined as a hyperlink, pressing <**Ctrl**> and clicking on it will take you directly to the target location.

Manoeuvres

1. Open **References**. Various types of reference are to be created.
2. Position the cursor after **Elizabeth I** in paragraph 1. Type **(Page** .
3. Select **Insert | Reference | Cross-reference**. From **Reference type** choose **Bookmark**. A list of all the bookmarks can now be seen.
4. From **Insert reference to** select **Page number** and **For which bookmark** highlight **Elizabeth**.
5. Make sure **Insert as hyperlink** is checked, so that a dynamic link between the reference and the referenced text will be created and click on **Insert** to create the cross-reference. Click **Close**.

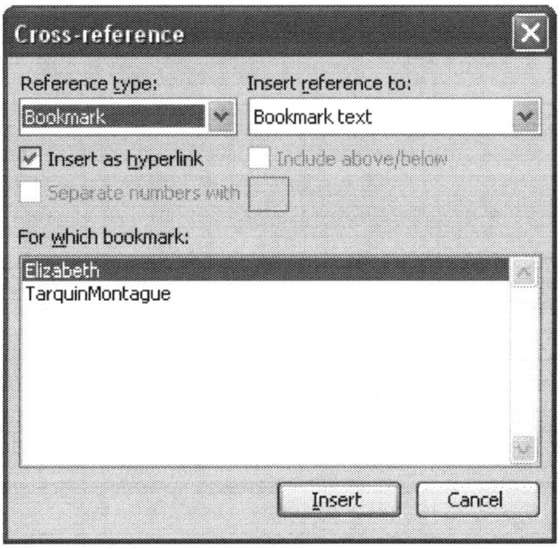

6. Next to **(Page** the number **2** appears. Enter **)** after the number 2.
7. Position the mouse pointer over the cross-reference page number, which has just been inserted - a caption appears, because the cross-reference was inserted as a hyperlink. If the caption does not appear, select **Tools | Options | View** and check **ScreenTips**, then click **OK**.

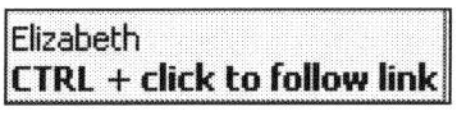

8. Hold down <**Ctrl**> and click once to move to the associated paragraph.

*After moving to a cross-reference, the **Back** button, , on the **Web** toolbar can be used to move back to the previous position in the document.*

Driving Lesson 41 - Continued

9. On page 1, place the cursor in the list after **The House**. Again type **(Page** and display the **Cross-reference** dialog box.
10. This time select **Heading** as the **Reference type** and insert the reference to **Page number**. Select the heading **The House**, click **Insert** and **Close**. Complete the reference with a closing bracket **)**.
11. Create references like this for the remaining items in the list.
12. On page 1, place the cursor at the end of paragraph 1 and type **See further information in paragraph number** .
13. Insert a cross reference to a **Numbered item**, in **Insert reference to** a **Paragraph number** and to go to item **1** in the list.

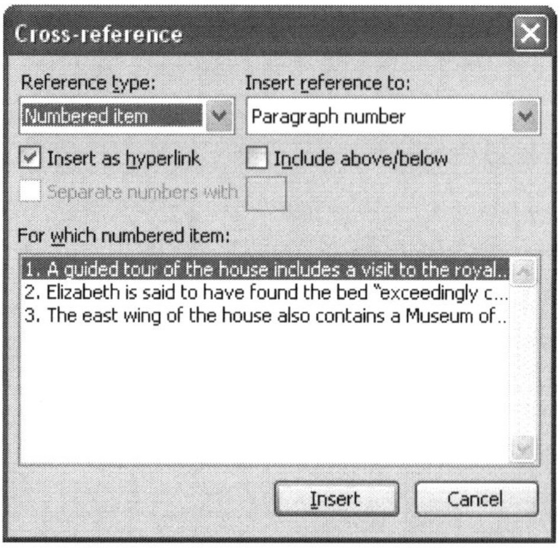

14. Click **Insert**, close the **Cross-reference** dialog box and complete the sentence with a full stop.
15. After the list, type **See opening times, page** and insert a cross reference to a **Table**, reference to **Page number** and choose the caption **Table 1**.
16. Move to page 2. Place the cursor after **from the tower** in the last paragraph, add a space and insert a cross reference.
17. Choose **Figure** as the **Reference type**, insert the reference to **Entire caption** and choose the caption **Figure 2**.
18. Try out the cross references.
19. Save the document as **Crossref** and leave it open.

*To delete a cross-reference the field codes must be viewed. Select **Tools | Options** and the **View** tab. Check the **Field codes** box and click **OK**. Position the cursor in front of the cross reference to be deleted and press <**Delete**> twice. Remember to turn the field codes off after deleting the cross-reference.*

Driving Lesson 42 - Adding Numbered Captions

Park and Read

Captions can be added individually to objects such as graphs, images and tables. They can also be set up to be automatically applied, so that when a graph, etc., is inserted, it is automatically numbered. Once captions have been entered in this way a **table of figures/captions** can also be created.

Manoeuvres

1. With **Crossref** still open from the previous lesson, move to the end of the document and press <**Enter**> to create a blank line.
2. Insert a 3 x 3 table and select it.
3. Select **Insert | Reference | Caption**. From **Label** choose **Table**. The caption can be positioned above or below the item. Select **Above selected item** in the **Position** box.

4. Click **OK**. The caption **Table 2** appears above the table, because **Table 1** already exists.
5. Scroll up the document and position the cursor above the **Pets' Corner** paragraph and insert another 3 x 3 table.
6. Keeping the cursor within the table, select **Insert | Reference | Caption**, ensure **Label** shows **Table**.
7. To change the caption text, enter **Events timetable** after the existing text in **Caption**. Click **OK**. The caption **Table 1 Events timetable** appears.
8. Scroll down to the other tables and notice they have been renumbered.
9. The figures in the document all have captions except the one in the **Pets Corner** paragraph. Click on this figure and select **Insert | Reference | Caption**.
10. Click the **Label** drop down, the available options are; **Equation**, **Figure** and **Table**. **Figure** is selected initially as the other captions are figures in the document. Select **Figure**.

Driving Lesson 42 - Continued

11. Another label is required, click the **New Label** button, enter **Image** and click **OK**.
12. Click **OK** to add the new caption label to the figures.
13. To delete a caption label, select the **Image 3** caption, display the **Caption** dialog box, with **Image** displayed click the **Delete Label** button. The label is deleted and the caption reverts back to **Figure**. Set the position to **Below selected item**.
14. Click **OK**. The figure becomes **Figure 3** and all subsequent figures are renumbered accordingly.
15. To change the caption format, select any figure, select **Insert | Reference | Caption**, and click the **Numbering** button.
16. In the **Caption Numbering** dialog box, drop down the **Format** options and select **A,B,C, ...**
17. Click **OK**, then click **OK** again to close the **Caption** dialog box. All figure captions are changed.
18. **AutoCaptions** make it possible to automatically insert a caption relating to an object as soon as it is inserted into a document. Select **Insert | Reference | Caption** then **AutoCaption**.

19. Scroll down the list and check **Microsoft Word Table**.
20. Click **OK** and insert a table anywhere in the document. Notice that a caption has automatically been created for it.
21. Apart from the table showing opening times, delete the other tables and captions. Ensure that the document still has only 4 pages.
22. The remaining table has not been renumbered and so has the wrong caption number. To update it, select the caption and press <**F9**>.

*If more than one table, figure, etc. needs renumbering, select the whole document and press <**F9**>. All captions in the document will be renumbered.*

23. Save the document and leave it open.

Driving Lesson 43 - Creating a Table of Figures

Park and Read

A table of figures is a list of the captions for pictures, charts, graphs, slides, or other illustrations in a document, along with the page numbers where they appear.

Manoeuvres

1. Use the **Crossref** document for this exercise.

2. Place the cursor on page 1, beneath the list and the opening times reference.

3. Change the font to **Arial 12pt** bold, not italic. Type **Table of Figures** and press <**Enter**>.

4. Select **Insert | Reference | Index and Tables** and the **Table of Figures** tab. Select **Distinctive** from **Formats** and from **Caption label** select **Figure**.

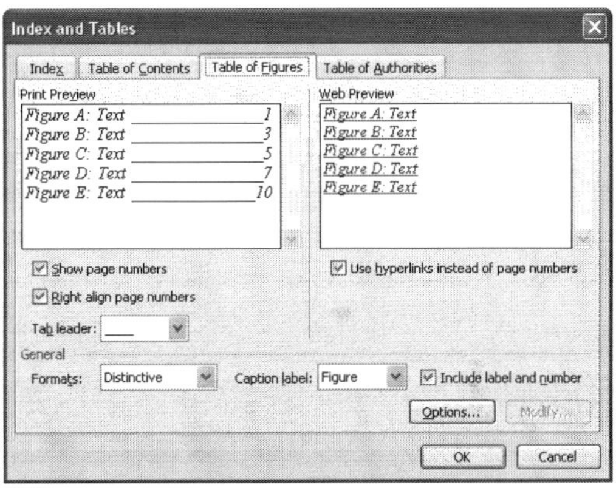

5. Click **OK**.

6. Use <**Ctrl**> and click to test the links.

7. Remove the caption from **Figure B**.

8. To renumber the remaining figures press <**Ctrl A**> then press <**F9**>.

9. To update the table, place the cursor in front of **Figure A** of the **Table of Figures**.

10. Press <**F9**> and select **Update entire table**.

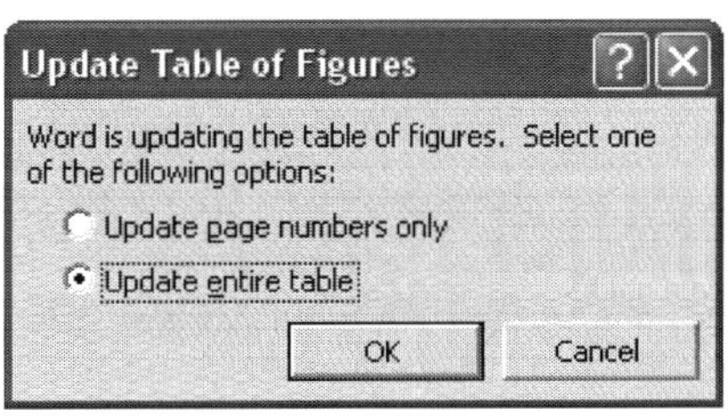

11. Click **OK**. Save the changes to the document and leave it open.

Driving Lesson 44 - Creating Index Entries

Park and Read

An **index** shows the position of selected words or phrases in a document. Text required for inclusion in the index must be specifically marked before the index can be created.

Once styles and captions have been created in a document and cross-referencing and index entries have been marked, it is a simple process to create tables for the entries.

Manoeuvres

1. Use **Crossref**. Highlight the first occurrence of the word **house** in the first paragraph.

2. Select **Insert | Reference | Index and Tables**. Make sure the **Index** tab is selected.

3. Click on **Mark Entry** to display the **Mark Index Entry** dialog box. Ensure **Current page** is selected from **Options**.

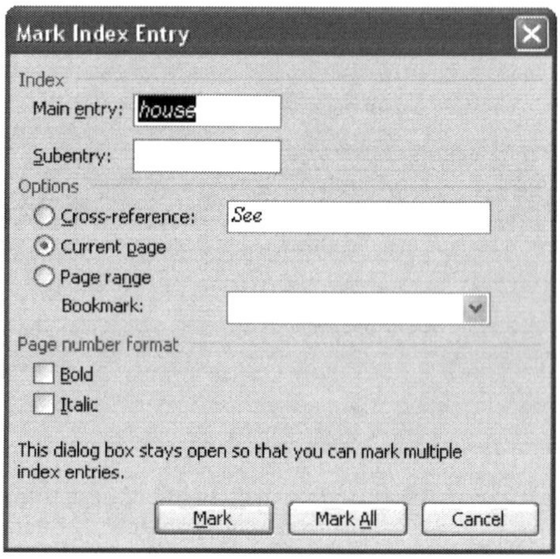

*To mark an index entry quickly, select the text and press <**Alt Shift X**>.*

*Indexes can also be marked by entering all the words to be indexed in a separate document. Save the document and from the **Index** tab, select **AutoMark**. Select the created file and Word will automatically index every occurrence of the word(s).*

4. Click **Mark All** to create an index entry for the first occurrence of **house**. In each paragraph. The index entry is shown as a field, beginning with **XE**. Click the **Show/Hide** button, ¶, if necessary to show the index entries.

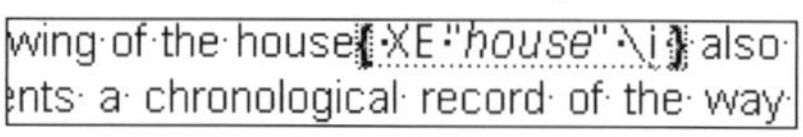

*Indexes are case sensitive: **House** is not the same as **house**.*

Driving Lesson 44 - Continued

5. Click **Close** to remove the dialog box. Scroll through the document. An index mark appears next to every occurrence of **house**.

6. Go to paragraph 2 on page 1 and highlight the word **gardens**.

7. Press <**Shift Alt X**> to view the **Mark Index Entry** dialog box.

8. Click **Mark All** and **Close** the dialog box.

9. Scroll down the document and create index entries for: **Elizabeth**, **Pets' Corner**, **shop** and **tea room** (do not use the entries in the Table of figures or the paragraph titles).

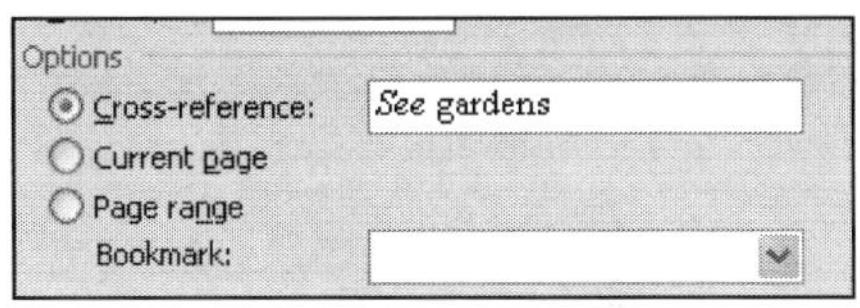

10. On page 2 highlight the word **tower** and press <**Shift Alt X**>.

11. In the **Mark Index Entry** dialog box, select **Cross-reference** in the **Options** area and after ***See***, type in **gardens**.

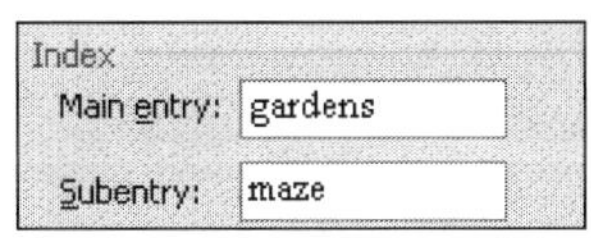

12. On page 3 highlight the word **maze** and press <**Shift Alt X**>.

13. In the **Mark Index Entry** dialog box, type **gardens** as the **Main entry** and **maze** as the **Subentry**.

14. Save the document as **Index**.

15. To create the index, insert a page break at the end of the document and type **Index** on the new page. Format **Index** as **Heading 1**.

16. On a new line below this heading select **Insert | Reference | Index and Tables** and the **Index** tab.

17. Set **Columns** to **1** and select the **Fancy** format. Click **OK** to create an **Index table**. Notice how **maze** is shown as a subentry of **gardens**, and how the entry for **tower** shows **See gardens**. A cross reference has been created from the index.

18. Move to the first index entry **tea rooms** and if you don't see the **XE** fields, click **Show/Hide**, ¶.

19. To edit the index entry, change the text inside the quotation marks to **cafe**.

20. Select the index entry for **tower** in the text, select the entire field including the brackets **{ }**, and then press <**Delete**>.

21. To update the index to show the edited entries, click anywhere in the table and press <**F9**>.

22. Close the document, saving the changes.

Driving Lesson 45 - Revision: Referencing

This is not an ECDL test. Testing may only be carried out through certified ECDL test centres. This covers the features introduced in this section. Try not to refer to the preceding Driving Lessons while completing it.

1. Open the document **Aurora Formatted**.
2. Create endnotes in the **i,ii,iii** style for the following areas:

    Greenland page 1 paragraph 2 – **said by many to be the best place to view the lights**.

    Eskimos page 2 – **native Inuit people**.
3. Move the insertion point back into the document. Amend the second endnote, adding the text **to give them their proper name**.
4. Save the document as **Aurora Formatted2** and close it.
5. Open **Stately Home Headings** and at the top of the document, create a table of contents based on the currently formatted headings.
6. Insert a page break before **The Gardens** on page 1. Now update the table of contents.
7. Create an index at the end of the document, using all headings as index marks.
8. Save the document as **Stately Home3** and close it.
9. Open the document **Predators** and create a bookmark for each heading in bold print.
10. Create an additional bookmark to the text **The grey nurse shark** in the **Methods of Reproduction** paragraph.
11. Insert a cross-reference from the first sentence of the **Diet** paragraph to the **The grey nurse shark** bookmark text.
12. Set up **Microsoft Word Picture** automatic captioning.
13. Insert an appropriate graphic from **Clip Art** after the **Teeth** section and a second graphic after the **Sight** paragraph.
14. Create a table of figures at the front of the document.
15. Save the document as **Jaws** and close it.

If you experienced any difficulty completing this Revision refer back to the Driving Lessons in this section. Then redo the Revision.

Once you are confident with the features, complete the Record of Achievement Matrix referring to the section at the end of the guide. Only when competent move on to the next Section.

Section 7 Collaborative Editing

By the end of this Section you should be able to:

Add and Remove Comments

Edit Comments

Track Changes to a Document

Accept or Reject Changes

Compare and Merge Documents

To gain an understanding of the above features, work through the **Driving Lessons** in this **Section**.

For each **Driving Lesson**, read the **Park and Read** instructions, without touching the keyboard, then work through the numbered steps of the **Manoeuvres** on the computer. Complete the **Revision Exercise(s)** at the end of the section to test your knowledge.

Driving Lesson 46 - Adding/Editing Comments

Park and Read

Comments are used to make notes on a document. They are usually for on-screen reference but can be printed if required.

Manoeuvres

1. Open **Predators**.
2. In the first paragraph highlight the word **Mediterranean**. Select **Insert | Comment**.
3. In the **Comment** balloon at the right of the screen, enter **It has recently been discovered that the Great White Shark comes here to breed**. Click away from the comment area.
4. Brackets have been added to **Mediterranean** and a dashed line leads to the comment.

*Balloons are only displayed in **Print** or **Web Layout View**. In **Normal View** or if balloons are not used, comments are entered in a pane at the bottom of the screen and the comment will appear when the mouse rests over the word in brackets. To remove the balloon option, select **Tools | Options | Track Changes** remove the check from **Use balloons in Print and Web Layout** and click **OK**.*

5. Find **cut** in the second paragraph and highlight it. Select **Insert | Comment** and type **These cuts can result in shark attack**. Click away from the comment.
6. Highlight the word **Mediterranean** in the first paragraph. After a few seconds a note appears, with information about the comment.

*To hide comments from view, select **View | Markup**. Select the same option again to restore them.*

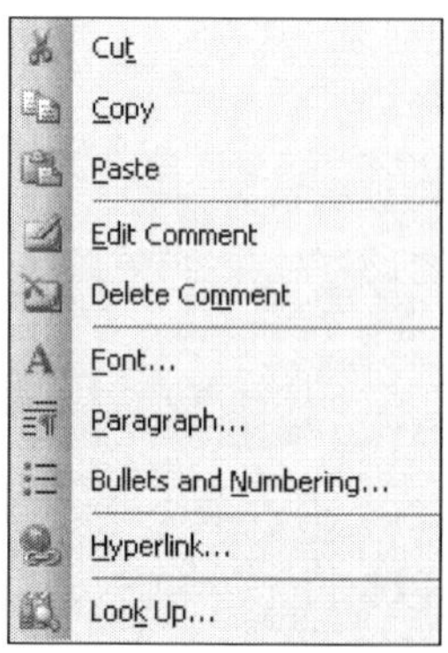

7. Right click on the word **Mediterranean**. Select **Edit Comment** from the shortcut menu.
8. The cursor moves to the comment balloon. Edit the comment to **The Great White Shark uses the area as a nursery**. Click away from the comment.
9. Right click over the **cut** comment. Select **Delete Comment** from the shortcut menu to delete the comment.
10. Save the document as **Comments** and then close it.

Driving Lesson 47 - Tracking Changes

Park and Read

When a document is being developed, particularly if it is being revised by different people, it is very useful to have all the amendments clearly visible within the document. By tracking changes to a document, it is possible to see where, when and who made the changes to it. Text that has been amended, added to or deleted from a document is shown.

Manoeuvres

1. Open **CiA**. This is a draft version of the document.
2. Select **Tools | Track Changes**. The **Status bar** shows **TRK** to denote that tracking is activated, and the **Reviewing** toolbar is displayed.
3. At the end of the first paragraph, enter **Materials are used worldwide.**
4. Notice that the words have been coloured. This denotes that the text has been added to the document.
5. Delete **to meet the needs of the client** on the last line of the third paragraph. The text appears in a balloon to show it has been deleted.

*In **Normal** view, deleted text is shown as strikethrough.*

6. Go to the end of the document.
7. Start a new paragraph and enter the following text: **For more information ring 0191 549 5002.**
8. Notice how the amended areas are noted in the left margin.
9. Save the document as **Tracking** but do not close it.

*Changes to tracking marks can be made by selecting **Tools | Options | Track Changes**.*

Driving Lesson 48 - Accepting and Rejecting Changes

Park and Read

Once changes have been tracked in a document, it is possible to view each change and either accept it or reject it. If the change is rejected, the text reverts to its original state. This is very useful when creating a joint report, or similar document.

A common scenario is for an author to create a report or similar document, then have it reviewed by one or more people. By tracking changes, the author can see which changes to the document have been suggested and decide whether to include them in the final version.

Manoeuvres

1. Use **Tracking** for this lesson and move to the top of the document.
2. Make sure the **Reviewing** toolbar is visible. If not, select **View | Toolbars | Reviewing**.
3. Click **Next**, to move to the first change.
4. In **Print Layout** view the deletions are shown in balloons. Place the cursor over the highlighted change and a caption is displayed showing details of the change.
5. Switch to **Normal** view.
6. Click **Show**, then **Reviewing Pane**. Notice how the pane at the bottom of the screen states what has been changed, by whom and when.
7. To accept the change, i.e. accept the added text, click on **Accept Change**, .
8. Click again. The next change is highlighted. Accept this change.
9. Click again. **Reject** the last change by clicking **Reject Change**, .
10. Notice that no text is now highlighted. This is because all the changes have been either accepted or rejected.
11. Click **Track Changes**, , to turn the tracking off and to be able to edit the text normally. **TRK** should not now be highlighted on the **Status Bar**.
12. Click to remove the **Reviewing Pane** across the bottom of the screen.
13. Save the document as **Final** before closing it.

Driving Lesson 49 - Compare and Merge

Park and Read

When reviewed documents are returned, the amendments must be checked and incorporated into the original. Two documents, the original and the edited versions, can be compared, to identify any differences at a glance. Input from several reviewers can be merged then processed in one operation.

Manoeuvres

1. Open the document **Review** and ensure the **Reviewing** toolbar is displayed. Assume for this exercise that you have sent copies of the original document to two colleagues for review, and they have returned the results as **R1** and **R2**.
2. Select **Tools | Compare and Merge Documents**.
3. Locate the folder containing the supplied data files and select **R1**.
4. From the **Merge** button drop down arrow, select **Merge into new document**. The changes are shown in a different colour to the rest of the text.
5. Repeat these steps to compare and merge **R2** but merge into the current document.
6. Amendments from both reviewers are now included in the one document, but have been given different colours to differentiate between them and the original text. Move the pointer over the added text in the first paragraph of the combined document.
7. The first colour represents amendments from user Bob. Move the pointer over the added text in the second paragraph (shown in a different colour). The second colour represents amendments from user Ian Chapman.
8. From the **Reviewing** toolbar, select each option in turn from the **Display for Review** drop down list to see how the view of the document changes.
9. With the display **Final Showing Markup** selected, click the drop down arrow on the **Accept Change** button,  and select **Accept All Changes in Document**. All tracking marks are removed. Save the file as **Reviewed**.
10. Assume the file is sent out for another review and a new version has been returned. Compare and merge the document with **R3** into the current document.
11. Accept all the changes, then save the document as **Reviewed** again.
12. Close the documents **Reviewed** and **Review**.

Driving Lesson 50 - Revision: Collaborative Editing

This is not an ECDL test. Testing may only be carried out through certified ECDL test centres. This covers the features introduced in this section. Try not to refer to the preceding Driving Lessons while completing it.

1. Open the document **Colorado**.
2. Set it up to track changes.
3. Insert a bold, centred **16pt** heading: **Colorado**.
4. Change the font size of the remainder of the text to **12pt**.
5. Make the first paragraph italic.
6. At the end of the final paragraph, enter **This natural wonder attracts hundreds of thousands of tourists annually**.
7. In the final paragraph, enter a comment after **marine sediment**, with the text **many fossils of sea creatures have been found**.
8. Work through the changes, accepting all apart from the inserted text, which should be rejected.
9. Close the document without saving.
10. Which feature allows you to see changes made to a reviewed document, within the original?

*See the **Answers** section at the end of the guide.*

If you experienced any difficulty completing this Revision refer back to the Driving Lessons in this section. Then redo the Revision.

Once you are confident with the features, complete the Record of Achievement Matrix referring to the section at the end of the guide. Only when competent move on to the next Section.

Section 8
Document Security

By the end of this Section you should be able to:

Password Protect a Document

Change Passwords

Remove Password Protection

To gain an understanding of the above features, work through the **Driving Lessons** in this **Section**.

For each **Driving Lesson**, read the **Park and Read** instructions, without touching the keyboard, then work through the numbered steps of the **Manoeuvres** on the computer. Complete the **Revision Exercise(s)** at the end of the section to test your knowledge.

Driving Lesson 51 - Password Protection

Park and Read

Passwords can be assigned to certain documents to restrict access to them. This is particularly important if a computer is shared or is on a network where it can be accessed by other users.

Passwords can be used to control whether a document can be opened or modified. A document can also be protected, so that only tracked changes or comments may be added. Be careful, as without the password, access to the document will not be allowed; make sure to use a password that will not be forgotten.

Manoeuvres

1. Open the document **Articles**.
2. To add a password, select **File | Save As | Tools | Security Options**.
3. Locate **File encryption options for this document** and enter **stories** as the password in **Password to open**.

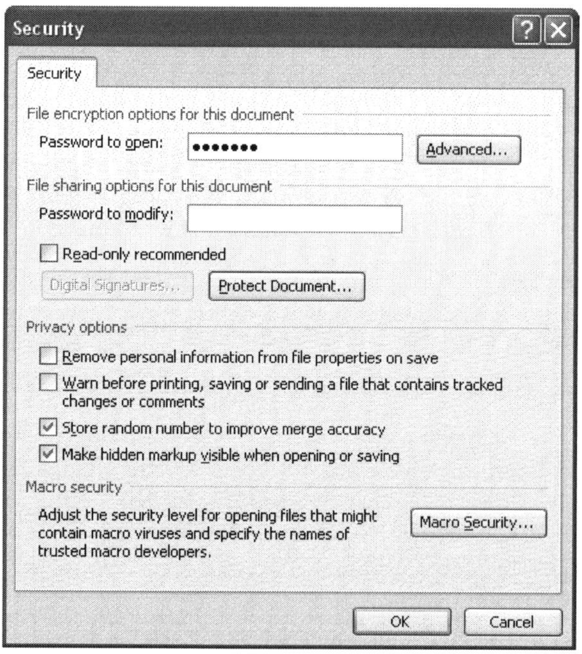

To set a password that will be required specifically to allow modification of the document, enter it in the ***File sharing options*** *area.*

Driving Lesson 51 - Continued

4. Click **OK**. Re-enter the same password in the **Reenter password to open** box, click **OK** and save the document as **Password**.

5. Close the document.

6. Open the document **Password** using the password **stories** to check whether it worked. Close the document.

7. Open the document **Colorado**.

8. Changes within a document can also be controlled and optionally passwords added. Select **View | Task Pane** and select **Protect Document** from the task pane drop down.

9. The **Protect Document** task pane is displayed. In section **2**, check **Allow only this type of editing in the document** and select **Comments** from the drop down list.

10. Click **Yes**, **Start Enforcing Protection**.

11. Add the password **pass** and re-enter the same password. Click **OK**.

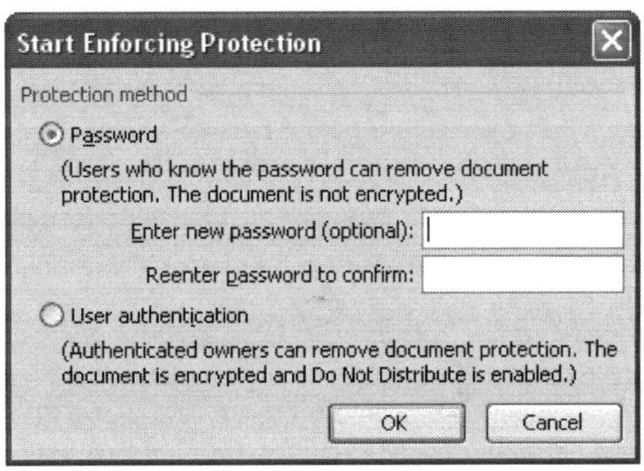

12. Save the document as **Locked**. This will allow a user to add comments, but not change the document in any other way.

13. Try to delete some text. You are unable to because only the addition of comments is allowed.

14. Insert the comment **I can't change this** after the first paragraph.

15. In the task pane, click **Stop Protection**. Enter the password, **pass** and click **OK**.

16. The document protection is removed. Try changing some text, there are no restrictions.

17. In the task pane under **Editing restrictions** select the **Tracked changes** option from the drop down list.

18. Click **Yes, Start Enforcing Protection**, add the password **pass** and re-enter the same password. Click **OK**.

19. Change one word in the text, this will be allowed but it will automatically generate tracking.

20. Save the document using the same file name and then close it.

Driving Lesson 52 - Removing and Changing Passwords

Park and Read

If it is decided to change or remove a password, follow the same general steps as for adding a password. The original password is always required to access the document before any changes can be made, and the document must be saved after the password is changed.

Manoeuvres

1. Open the document **Password** using the password **stories**.
2. A rumour is circulating that someone has accessed the document. For security reasons, change to a different password using **File | Save As | Tools | Security Options**.

*Password options are also available from **Tools | Options | Security**.*

3. In the **Password to open** area, enter a new password and click **OK**. Re-enter the password and click **OK**.
4. Save and then close the document.
5. Scandal is imminent - the document has been released to a rival newspaper. Reopen the document and remove the password by deleting the contents in the **Password to open** box.
6. Save the document and close it.
7. Open the document **Locked**.
8. From the **Protect Document** task pane, click **Stop Protection**.
9. Enter the password, **pass** and click **OK**. This removes document protection.
10. Save the document with the same name.
11. Check that the document is no longer password protected and can be edited by making a small change.
12. Save the document and then close it.

Passwords can only be changed when the document is open and can only be opened with the password. Therefore, passwords cannot be accidentally changed.

Driving Lesson 53 - Revision: Document Security

This is not an ECDL test. Testing may only be carried out through certified ECDL test centres. This covers the features introduced in this section. Try not to refer to the preceding Driving Lessons while completing it.

1. Open the document **Articles**.
2. Save the document as **Top Secret**.
3. Apply a password to open it.
4. Test the password.
5. Change the password to **Secret**.
6. Protect the document so that no edits may be made without the changes being tracked.
7. Test the password again.
8. Remove the password and document protection.
9. Save the document using the same filename.
10. Close the document.

If you experienced any difficulty completing this Revision refer back to the Driving Lessons in this section. Then redo the Revision.

Once you are confident with the features, complete the Record of Achievement Matrix referring to the section at the end of the guide. Only when competent move on to the next Section.

Section 9 Master Documents & Templates

By the end of this Section you should be able to:

Create a Master Document

Create a Subdocument

Add or Remove a Subdocument

Modify a Template

To gain an understanding of the above features, work through the **Driving Lessons** in this **Section**.

For each **Driving Lesson**, read the **Park and Read** instructions, without touching the keyboard, then work through the numbered steps of the **Manoeuvres** on the computer. Complete the **Revision Exercise(s)** at the end of the section to test your knowledge.

Driving Lesson 54 - Creating a Master Document

Park and Read

A **master document** can be used when a report is too long to be maintained as one document. **Subdocuments** can be created, then inserted into the master document. They can be printed individually or altogether. They can also be used to create tables of contents. Master documents can be used in **Outline View** to organise headings, contents and indexes.

An example of a master document/subdocument structure could be a book, where the master document contains the title and the chapter headings, and each individual chapter is in a separate subdocument.

Manoeuvres

1. Start a new document and switch to **Outline** view.
2. Notice the **Master Document** buttons at the right of the **Outlining** toolbar.

*If necessary click **Master Document View**,*  *, to display all the buttons.*

3. With the style as **Heading 1**, enter the title **The Book I Always Wanted to Write**.
4. Press <**Enter**>.
5. Change the style of the next line to **Heading 2**.
6. Type in the text **Chapter One**. The **Master Document** is now ready to have subdocuments added.

7. Leave the document open and move to the next Driving Lesson.

Driving Lesson 55 - Creating a Subdocument

Park and Read

A **subdocument** is created and saved in the same way as a normal document. Once a subdocument is inserted/created in a master document, the two documents are linked. This allows the subdocument to be opened and changed individually, or through the master document. A master document can also help members of a workgroup to create and update parts of a long document.

Manoeuvres

1. With the insertion point still at the end of the **Chapter One** text, select **Create Subdocument** . This places the chapter heading inside a grey outline, defining the subdocument.

2. Save the document as **My Book**. The subdocument will automatically be saved as **Chapter One**.

3. Double click on the subdocument icon to open **Chapter One**. Underneath the title (using the **Normal** style) enter **I was born in the early summer of 19##**. Click on **Save**.

4. Using the **Taskbar**, switch back to **My Book** to view the reflected changes. Close both documents, saving if prompted.

5. Open **My Book**. Note how the subdocument is now displayed only as a file name, e.g.

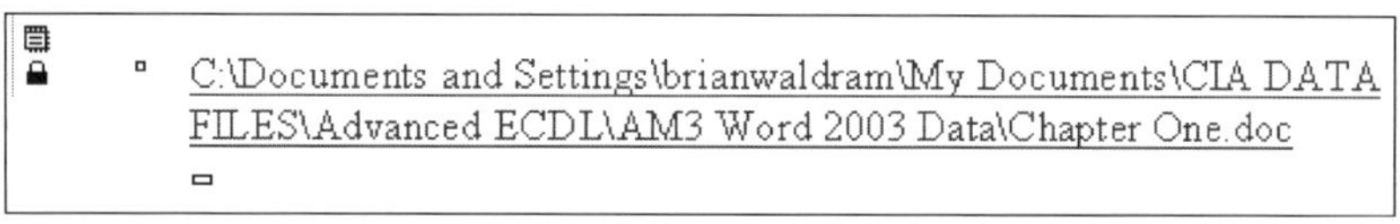

6. Move the pointer over the file name, hold down <**Ctrl**> and click once on the file name to open the document.

7. Close it again. Click on **Expand Subdocuments** . All the entered text is now displayed. Text can also be entered here.

Driving Lesson 55 - Continued

8. Click beside the last text entry icon and enter **Chapter Two**. Make this a subdocument by clicking **Create Subdocument**, .

9. Save **My Book**.

10. Double click on **Chapter Two**'s subdocument icon and enter the text **I went to school at...**. Close and save **Chapter Two**.

11. Collapse the subdocuments using . The **Master Document** appears similar to the diagram below.

Subdocument locked

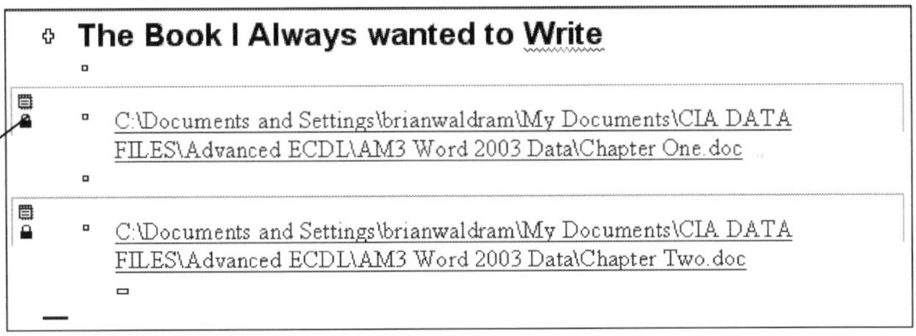

12. Subdocuments are usually **locked** when they are not to be modified, i.e. are read-only. However, in this case, expand the documents and the locks will be opened.

13. Click on **Master Document** to view where the **Section Breaks** (dotted lines) occur. Note that they are before and after each subdocument. **Section Breaks** were covered in a previous Driving Lesson.

*If **Show/Hide** is on the **Section Breaks** are always shown.*

14. Click on again and collapse the subdocuments. **Print Preview** the **Master Document** selecting **Yes** at the dialog box.

15. Close **Print Preview**, but leave **My Book** open.

Driving Lesson 56 - Adding and Removing a Subdocument

Park and Read

Previously created documents can be used as subdocuments.

Manoeuvres

1. Use the Master Document **My Book**, which should still be open from the previous Driving Lesson.
2. Click beside the last text entry icon and click the **Insert Subdocument** button, .
3. From the data files, select the document **Chapter 3** and click **Open**.

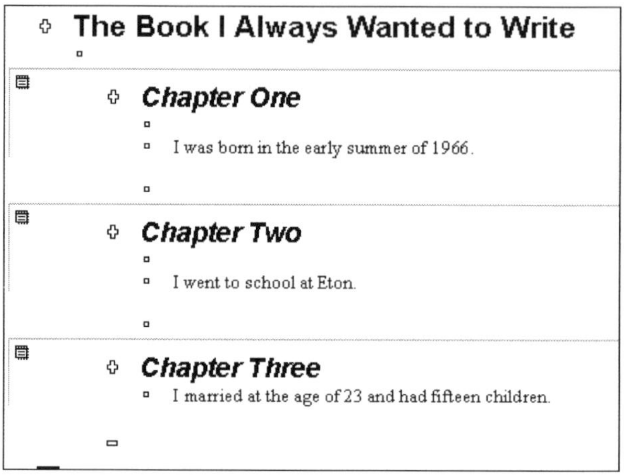

4. The document is inserted as a subdocument.
5. To delete the **Chapter 3** subdocument, first make sure the subdocuments are expanded.
6. Click on the **Chapter 3** subdocument icon and press <**Delete**> to remove it.

*Always check the **Breaks** when creating or adding sub documents. Inserted sub documents have **Next Page** breaks, created documents have **Continuous** breaks.*

7. Save and close **My Book**.

Driving Lesson 57 - Modifying a Template

Park and Read

A template is a special document that is used as the basis for creating other documents. It contains the necessary formatting and framework to ensure that all documents created from it are consistent in appearance. It is possible to change a template as desired after it has been created, in the same way as normal documents can be edited.

Manoeuvres

1. Open the document **CV**. Select **File | Save As** and change the **File name** to **CV template** and the **Save as type** to **Document Template**.
2. Click **Save**. The document is saved as a template to the **Templates** folder. Close the template.
3. Select **File | New** and under **Templates** select **On my computer** in the task pane.

4. Select **CV Template** and click **Template** under **Create New**. Click **OK**.
5. To apply a watermark, select **Format | Background | Printed Watermark**.

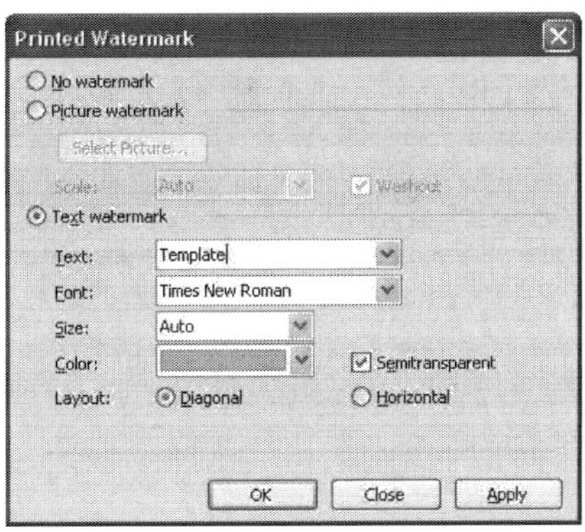

6. Select **Text watermark** and in the **Text** box enter **Template**.
7. Click **OK**.
8. Select all of the text in the document.
9. Change the font to **Book Antiqua**, or an alternative if this font is unavailable.
10. Select **File | Save As**. Change the name to **CV template** and save it to overwrite the original. The changes are saved in the same way as a normal *Word* document, to the **Templates** folder.
11. Close the template.
12. Select **File | New** and **On my computer** in the **Task Pane**. Don't open the template. It is to be deleted so that this Driving Lesson can be repeated on the same computer.
13. Right click on the **CV template** icon. Select **Delete** from the menu.
14. Select **Yes** at the prompt and click **Cancel** to close the dialog box.

Driving Lesson 58 - Revision: Master Documents and Templates

This is not an ECDL test. Testing may only be carried out through certified ECDL test centres. This covers the features introduced in this section. Try not to refer to the preceding Driving Lessons while completing it.

1. Create a master document from the following files: **Beverages**, **Cuisine** and **Deli**.
2. Remove any unwanted blank pages.
3. Save the master document as **Food and drink**.
4. Preview the master document then adjust the section breaks so that there are only three pages (you may need to switch views to do this).
5. Remove the subdocument **Deli**.
6. Save the changes to the master document.
7. Close it.
8. Open one of the prepared templates (in **Templates,** the **Letters and Faxes** tab) - the **Elegant Fax** as a template.
9. Add a text watermark (**CONFIDENTIAL**).
10. Save the amended template as **Watermarked Fax.dot** in the template location.
11. Delete the amended template.

If you experienced any difficulty completing this Revision refer back to the Driving Lessons in this section. Then redo the Revision.

Once you are confident with the features, complete the Record of Achievement Matrix referring to the section at the end of the guide. Only when competent move on to the next Section.

Section 10
Field Codes and Forms

By the end of this Section you should be able to:

Insert, Delete, Edit and Update Field Codes

Lock or Unlock a Field

Create and Edit a Form

Change Form Field Options

Protect and Delete Form Fields

To gain an understanding of the above features, work through the **Driving Lessons** in this **Section**.

For each **Driving Lesson**, read the **Park and Read** instructions, without touching the keyboard, then work through the numbered steps of the **Manoeuvres** on the computer. Complete the **Revision Exercise(s)** at the end of the section to test your knowledge.

Driving Lesson 59 - Working with Field Codes

Park and Read

Fields are used for two main purposes. Firstly to insert codes, which are then substituted with current information such as the date or the document title. Secondly, to define parts of a document which will accept data input, in a form for example. Form fields are described in a later Driving Lesson.

Manoeuvres

1. Open the document **Summary**. Select **File | Properties** and add your name to the document as **Author** and **Technical Report** as the **Title**. Click **OK**.
2. Add four blank lines to the top of the document. Click in the first blank line and select **Insert | Field**. The **Field** dialog box is displayed.
3. From the **Categories**, select **Document Information** and then select **Title** from **Field names**. Click **OK**.

*If a field code **{TITLE...}** is shown instead of the field content (**Technical Report**), press <**Alt F9**> to switch the view.*

4. On the second line insert the field name **Author**, and on the third line insert the field **FileSize**. Both fields from **Document Information**.
5. On the fourth line insert the field **Fill-in**, from the **Mail Merge** category. Specify a prompt of **Enter text**. Click **OK** and enter the text **Information**. Click **OK**.

***Fill-in** fields prompt for data to be entered whenever the field is updated. These are often used in templates and in mail merge applications.*

6. Select **View | Header and Footer**. With the cursor positioned in the **Header**, select **Insert | Field**. From **Categories** select **Document Information** and from **Field names** select **FileName**. Check the **Add path to filename** and click **OK** to add the **file name and path** field to the header.
7. Fields can be added easily using the **Header and Footer** toolbar. Click the **Switch between Header and Footer** button, .
8. Click the **Insert Time** button, , to insert the time as a field, tab to the right of the **Footer** and click the **Insert Date** button, , to insert the current date as a field.
9. Close the **Footer** using the **Close** button, or by double clicking on a blank area of the screen. Print a copy of the document.
10. Save the document as **Fields** and close it.

Driving Lesson 60 - Editing and Updating Field Codes

Park and Read

Some fields containing numerical information, for example the date or time, are updated automatically when printing, previewing or merging. Other fields are not. All fields can however be updated manually at any time by using the **<F9>** function key.

Manoeuvres

1. Open the document **Time**. Each of the four numbered lines contains a time field.

*Depending on the settings in **Tools | Options | View,** fields may be shown highlighted.*

2. Use **<Alt F9>** if necessary to make sure the time values are being shown rather than the field codes. Notice each value has a different format.

*Another way to switch between viewing field codes and field content is to select **Tools | Options | View**, and check or uncheck the **Field codes** option.*

3. Press **<Alt F9>** to view the field codes. Notice that each field was given a different format definition when it was inserted.
4. Press **<Alt F9>** again to view the time values. Notice they are not current.
5. To update a single field, the cursor must be within the field. Position the cursor inside the time field in line 1. Press **<F9>** to update the time.
6. Field codes themselves may be edited. Right click in the field on line 1.
7. Select **Edit Field** from the shortcut menu. The **Field** dialog box is displayed.
8. With **Time** selected from the **Field names** list, choose an **am/pm** format.
9. Click **OK**. The field now shows the current time in the chosen format.
10. Note all the time values which are displayed, then print out a single copy of the document. All dates and times are automatically updated, except for line 3 which is locked (see next Driving Lesson).

*To make sure that all fields are updated when printed, select **Tools | Options | Print** and ensure the **Update fields** box is checked.*

11. Leave the document open for the next Driving Lesson.

Driving Lesson 61 - Locking/Unlocking Fields

Park and Read

Sometimes fields may need to be fixed, i.e. not require updating. In order to fix a specific value in a field, the **Lock Field** key <**Ctrl F11**> is used.

Manoeuvres

1. Use the document **Time** for this Driving Lesson.
2. Wait for a minute then use <**F9**> to update the time in line 2.
3. Try using the same process to update the time on the line 3. This field has been locked; the time is fixed and will not be updated.
4. With the cursor still in the field on line 3, unlock the field by pressing <**Ctrl Shift F11**>.
5. Now use <**F9**> and the time will update successfully.
6. Highlight the time in line 4. Lock the field by pressing <**Ctrl F11**>.
7. Try updating the field using <**F9**>.
8. Now unlock the field by pressing <**Ctrl Shift F11**>. Use <**F9**> to update.
9. Field codes can be deleted easily. Select the time field in line 4, making sure the entire field is highlighted.
10. Press <**Delete**>. The field is removed.

Fields can be deleted in either view, ***Field code*** *or* ***Field content****.*

11. Close the document <u>without</u> saving.

Driving Lesson 62 - Creating and Editing Forms

Park and Read

Form Fields are created to enable data to be entered into a document, which is then called a form. They are special fields that will prompt for data entry when the form is displayed. The layout of the form is designed first, then the fields are created. The form must be protected before the fields will work.

Manoeuvres

1. Start a new document and enter the text as below:

   Memo

   To:
   From:
   Date:
   Subject:
   Urgent:

   Message:

2. Select all of the text and insert a left tab stop at **3cm**.
3. Position the cursor after **To:** and press <**Tab**> to move to the tab stop.
4. Select **View | Toolbars | Forms** to view the **Forms** toolbar.

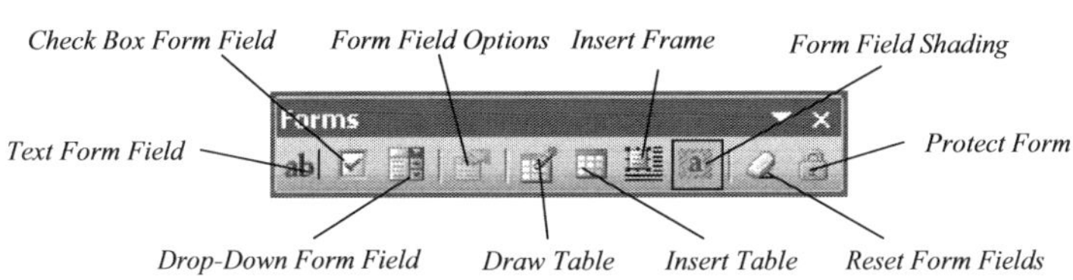

5. Click once on **Drop-Down Form Field**, , to create a field.
6. To delete the field, place the cursor in front of it and press <**Delete**> once to highlight the field, then again to delete it.
7. Now create the **Drop-Down Form Field** again, as it is needed for this form.
8. Leave the document open for the next Driving Lesson.

Driving Lesson 63 - Form Field Options

Park and Read

After a form field has been created, various options can be set to define the operation of the field, using form field options. For a **Drop-Down Form Field** for example, the choices given within the field have to be supplied. For a **Text Form Field**, the options include the type and format of entered data.

Manoeuvres

1. Using the document from the previous Driving Lesson, keep the cursor in the field and press the **Form Field Options** button, .
2. In **Drop-down item**, enter **Andrew Simpson**. Click on **Add**.
3. Enter the following names in the same manner: **Susan Peters**, **Ishmael Rampuri** and **Gita Patel**. Click **OK** to close the dialog box.

4. Click after **From** and press <**Tab**>. Click on the **Text Form Field** button, , to create a field. Click to display the options for the field and in **Default text**, enter your name and click **OK**.
5. Create a **Text Form Field** after **Date**. Click to define options for this field.
6. From **Type**, select **Current date** and in the **Date format** box, select **dd MMMM yyyy**. Click **OK**.
7. Place a **Text Form Field** after **Subject**. Click after **Urgent**, press <**Tab**>, then click on the **Check Box Form Field** button, .
8. Finally, create a **Text Form Field** on the line below **Message**.

Driving Lesson 63 - Continued

9. Define options for this field - click **Add Help Text**. Complete the box on the **Status Bar** tab as shown in the next diagram. This text will appear on the **Status Bar** when the text field is entered.

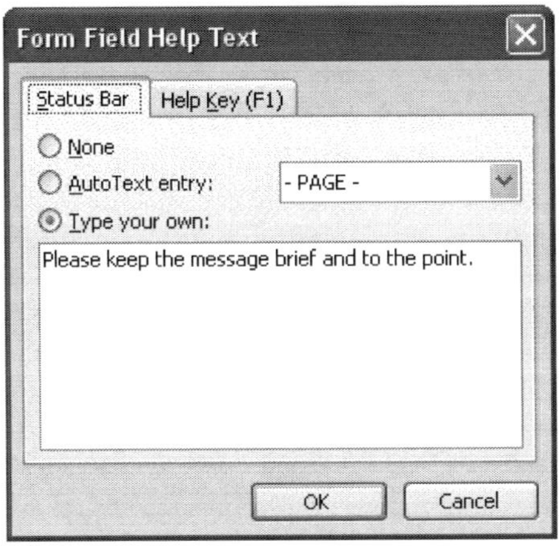

10. Select the **Help Key (F1)** tab. Select **Type your own** and enter **Don't ramble on!** This text will appear if <**F1**> is pressed when in the **Message** field.

11. Click **OK** and then **OK** again.

12. Press <**Alt F9**> to view the field codes.

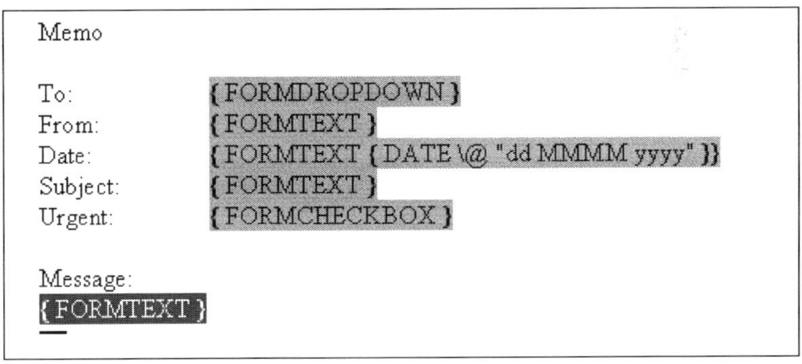

13. Press <**Alt F9**> again to see the field content.

14. Leave the document open for the next Driving Lesson.

Driving Lesson 64 - Protecting Form Fields

Park and Read

To allow the **Form Fields** to work on a form, the document must be protected. Once protected, data can only be entered in the **Form Fields**; no other changes will be allowed to the document.

Manoeuvres

1. Using the document from the previous Driving Lesson, click the **Protect Form** button, .
2. Save the document as **Form**.
3. Click in the first field - a drop down arrow appears.
4. Choose a name, then press <**Tab**> to move to the next field.
5. Your name is entered here already. Press <**Tab**> again to move to the **Subject**. Notice that the date is automatically set as the current date and cannot be changed.
6. In **Subject**, enter **Important Notice** then press <**Tab**>.
7. Click once in the field box next to **Urgent** to set the option.
8. Press <**Tab**> look at the **Status Bar** to see the **Help Text**. Press <**F1**>.
9. Click **OK** and enter the following message: **Please note that the budget has been cut by 10%, therefore I will need new costings urgently**.

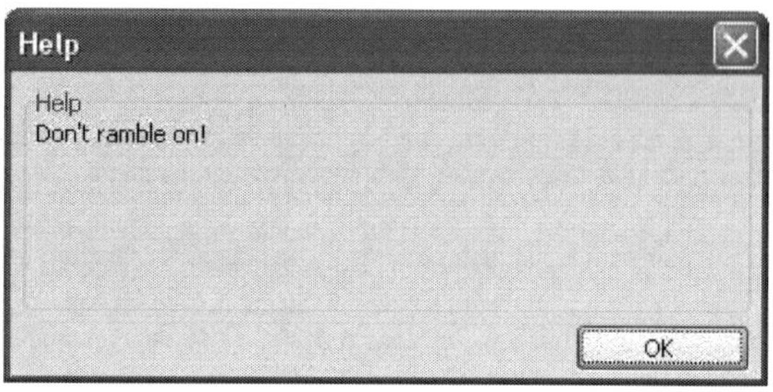

10. Try and change the word **Message** to **Comment**. It will not be allowed.
11. Press <**Alt F9**> to view the field codes. This will not be allowed.
12. Print the document, then save it as **Form2**.
13. Remove the protection by clicking the **Protect Form** button.
14. Press <**Alt F9**> to view the field codes. Select the whole of the field **{FORMCHECKBOX}** and press <**Delete**> to remove the field.
15. Close the document.

Driving Lesson 65 - Revision: Field Codes and Forms

This is not an ECDL test. Testing may only be carried out through certified ECDL test centres. This covers the features introduced in this section. Try not to refer to the preceding Driving Lessons while completing it.

1. Open the document **Predators**. Select **File | Properties** and make sure **Title**, **Subject** and **Author** are entered. Add them if necessary.
2. Use fields to insert the **Title** and **Author** on new lines immediately under the heading. Right align the fields.
3. On a new line at the end of the document, type **Report created on** and insert a date field.
4. Print the document then change the **Author** details in file properties to a different name and update the **Author** field in the document to reflect the change.
5. Change the **Title** field so that it shows the **FileName** instead. Lock the **Report created on** field so that it will never be updated.
6. Print the document again, save it as **Predators2**, and then close it
7. Start a new document to create a form inviting four colleagues to a meeting. Enter the text as below:

   Meeting Schedule

   To:

   From:

   Date:

   Time:

   Agenda:

   Reply req?
8. Set a tab at **4cm** for all of the text, then click after **To:** and press <**Tab**>. Insert a **Drop-Down Form Field** and enter the names of four colleagues (don't forget to use the **Form Field Options**).
9. Create **Text Form Fields** for **From: Date: Time:** and **Agenda**:.
10. Create a **Check Box Form Field** after **Reply req?** and **Protect** the form.
11. Select a name from the list for **To:**, enter your name in **From:**, enter today's date and the time as the current time. Check the check box.
12. Save the document as **Meeting** and close it. Close the **Forms** toolbar.

If you experienced any difficulty completing this Revision refer back to the Driving Lessons in this section. Then redo the Revision.
Once you are confident with the features, complete the Record of Achievement Matrix referring to the section at the end of the guide. Only when competent move on to the next Section.

Section 11
Mail Merge

By the end of this Section you should be able to:

Edit a Mail Merge Data Source

Sort and Query a Data Source

Use Ask and IF Fields

Use Different Data Sources

To gain an understanding of the above features, work through the **Driving Lessons** in this **Section**.

For each **Driving Lesson**, read the **Park and Read** instructions, without touching the keyboard, then work through the numbered steps of the **Manoeuvres** on the computer. Complete the **Revision Exercise(s)** at the end of the section to test your knowledge.

Driving Lesson 66 - Editing a Data Source

Park and Read

Often the same **Data Source** will be used with any number of **Main Documents** over a period of time, so it must be well planned and kept up to date. For example, a mailing list data source will have to be edited when contact details or addresses are changed.

Manoeuvres

1. Start a new, blank document, view the **Mail Merge** toolbar and the **Mail Merge Task Pane**.
2. At **Step 3 of 6** in the **Task Pane**, click on **Browse** and make sure **Look in** shows the location of the data files.
3. Select the **Clients** address list and click **Open**. The **Mail Merge Recipients** dialog box is displayed.
4. **Freda Jones**, the first person on the list, has left the country. Select her record. To remove it, click **Edit**. On the form that appears click **Delete Entry** and then **Yes** at the prompt.
5. Use the form to locate the record for **BB Computer Consultants**. They have moved to **49 George Street**. Amend the record accordingly.
6. Close the data form and click **OK** to close the **Mail Merge Recipients** dialog box. Close the document without saving.
7. Now open the document **Invitation**, which has a data source, **Contacts**, linked to it. At the message prompt click **Yes**. If a message appears about *Word* being unable to locate the data source, click **Find Data Source**. From **Look in**, select the location of the data files supplied. Select the **Contacts** data source and click **Open**.
8. Click the **Mail Merge Recipients** button,  from the **Mail Merge** toolbar to display the **Mail Merge Recipients** dialog box.
9. **George Murphy** (last on the list) has asked to be removed from the mailing list. Select his record. Click **Edit** to view the data form. Click **Delete Entry** and select **Yes** at the prompt.
10. Now click **Close** to return to the **Mail Merge Recipients** box. George Murphy's record has been removed.
11. Leave the **Mail Merge Recipients** dialog box open for the next Driving Lesson.

Driving Lesson 67 - Sorting a Data Source

Park and Read

It is possible to sort the records in a data source in ascending or descending alphabetical or numerical order. A data source can also be queried, so that only selected records are used in the mail merge, for example to send letters only to people in a particular city.

Manoeuvres

1. Make sure the **Mail Merge Recipients** dialog box is open.

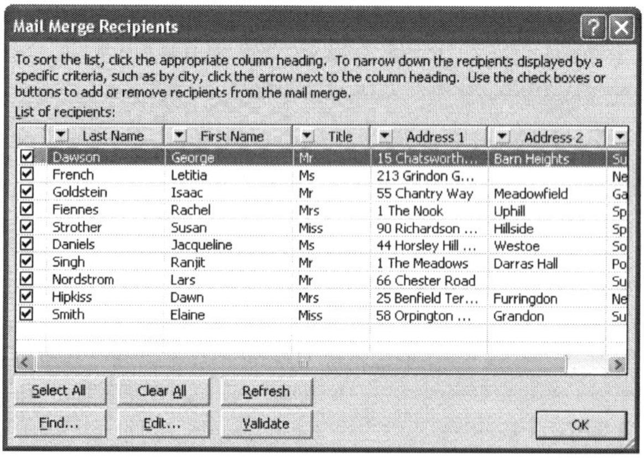

2. To sort the data alphabetically by surname, click the **Last Name** heading.
3. Notice how the records are now sorted in ascending alphabetical order.

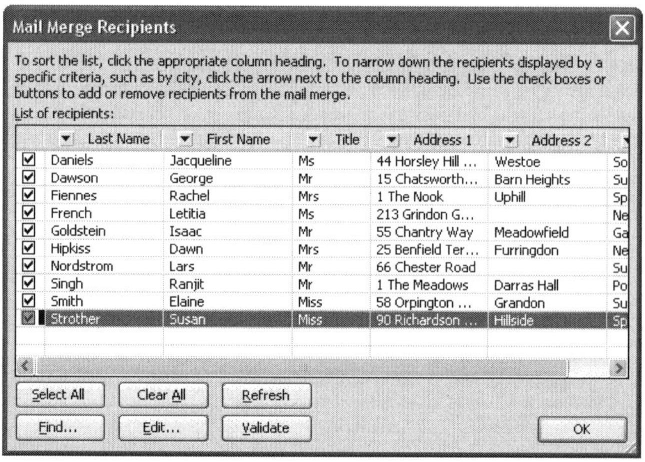

Driving Lesson 67 - Continued

4. To sort the records in descending alphabetical order of surname, click again on the **Last Name** header.

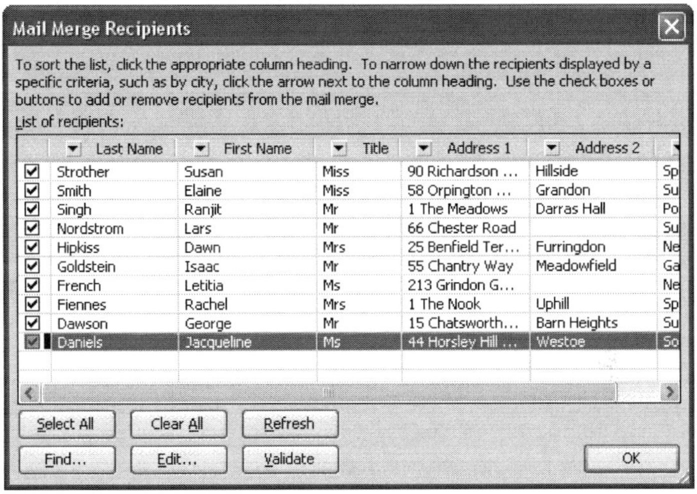

5. To **query** this data source and send letters to people living in **Sunderland**, but not to the others, use the scroll bar at the bottom of the **Mail Merge Recipients** dialog box to view the **City** heading.

6. Click the drop down arrow on the **City** heading.

7. Select **Sunderland** from the list. The arrow changes to blue to indicate that the list has been filtered. Click **OK**.

8. View the **Mail Merge Task Pane** and move to **Step 5 of 6** to preview the letters.

9. Move through the three letters using the **Task Pane** to see that they all live in **Sunderland**.

10. Leave **Invitation** open.

Driving Lesson 68 - Using Various Data Sources

Park and Read

When performing mail merge, you are not restricted to using data sources created in *Word*. It is also possible to use a table from an *Access* database, for example.

Manoeuvres

1. Use the main document **Invitation** for this Driving Lesson. Your colleague in Marketing has given you an address list containing new customers, to whom you want to send an invitation to the company's open day.
2. View the **Mail Merge** task pane at **Step 3 of 6**.
3. From the **Use an existing list** area of the task pane, click **Select a different list**.
4. Make sure **Files of type** at the bottom of the dialog box shows **All Data Sources** and **Look in** shows the location of the data files.
5. Select the **Clients** database and click **Open**. The list of contacts is displayed in the **Mail Merge Recipients** dialog box.
6. Widen the **Name** and **Town** fields, using the right edge of their headers.

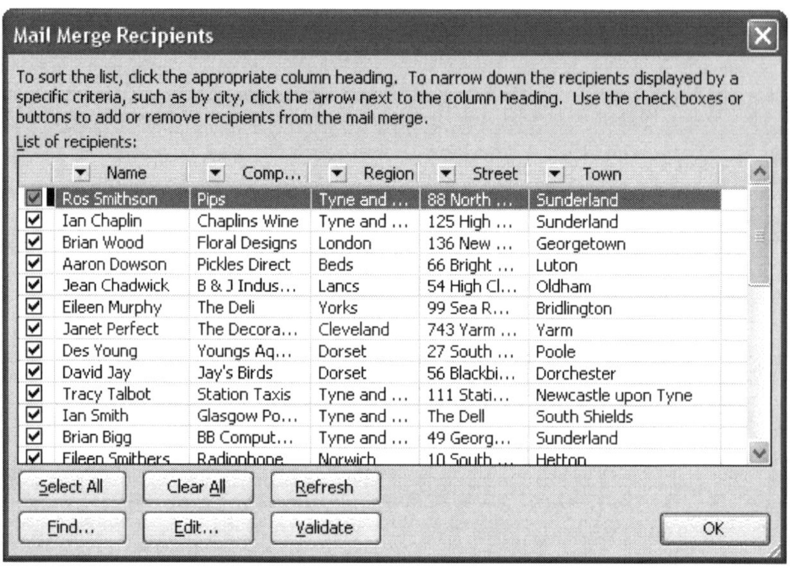

Driving Lesson 68 - Continued

7. Click **OK**. Now the main document has to be edited to contain the correct merge fields.

8. Delete the existing merge fields in the document.

9. Click on the **Insert Merge Fields** button, , on the **Mail Merge** toolbar to reveal the list of available fields in the *Access* table.

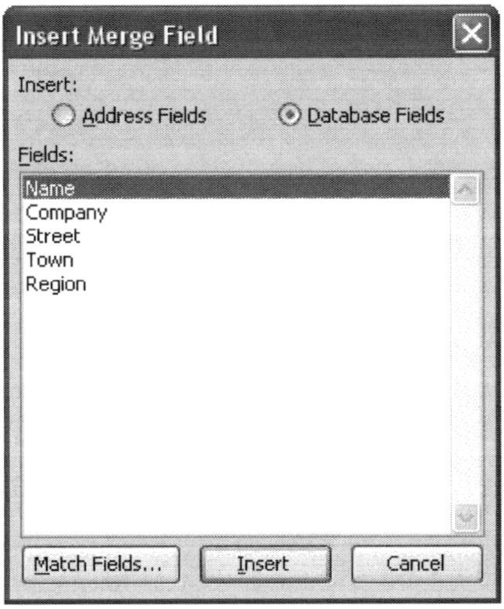

10. Place the new fields in the main document so that they match the diagram below.

«Name»
«Company»
«Street»
«Town»
«Region»

Dear «Name»

11. Move to **Step 5** on the **Task Pane** and preview the document to be merged, which should contain 30 letters.

12. Close **Invitation** <u>without</u> saving.

Driving Lesson 69 - Ask and IF Fields

Park and Read

Various special fields can be added to a mail merge main document in certain situations. For example, if a recipient lives in area A, send a letter with a money off coupon attached; if they live in area B, send just the letter. An **IF...then...else** field would be used to do this. If an **ASK** field is used in a mail merge main document, a prompt is displayed each time you merge a new data record. For example, to enter a date that will change every month, like a meeting or event. **Ask** must be used in conjunction with a **Ref** field to allow the results of the query to be displayed.

Manoeuvres

1. Open the document **Showroom** (linked to the data source **Customer List.mdb** in the same location).
2. This is a letter from a car showroom to promote new models to existing customers. Depending on their home address, they are invited to attend one of two possible locations.
3. Place the cursor between **to** and **on** and ensure the **Mail Merge** toolbar is displayed.
4. Click Insert Word Field and select **If...Then...Else**.
5. From **Field name** select **City** and ensure **Comparison** shows **Equal to**. Enter **Sunderland** in **Compare to**.
6. In **Insert this text**, type **Park Lane Showroom** and in **Otherwise insert this text**, type **North Road Showroom**.

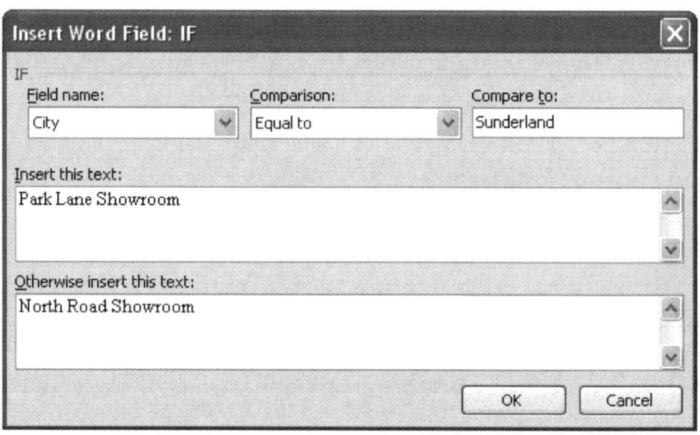

Driving Lesson 69 - Continued

7. Click **OK**. This means that any customers living in Sunderland will be invited to Park Lane Showroom, but those in Newcastle will be invited to North Road Showroom. The field can be formatted. Highlight the field text and change the font to **Arial** to match the other text.

8. View the **Mail Merge** task pane at step 5 of 6 and preview the letters to see the **IF** field in action.

9. Complete the merge (**Edit individual letters**), merging all and saving the merge file as **Carmerge**.

10. Close any open documents, saving the changes to **Showroom**.

11. Open the document **Event**, linked to the data source **Visitors.mdb**.

12. This mail merge will contain a date that varies. An **Ask** field needs to be used. As these fields work via bookmarks, one needs to be created where the field information is to be shown.

13. Click between **on** and **and** in paragraph 2 and select **Insert | Bookmark**.

14. Enter the bookmark name as **Event_Date** and click **Add**.

15. Click in front of **As one of our...** and click 

, this time choosing **Ask**.

*The location of the **Ask** field is not important, as it will not be seen in the finished document, but it must be before the first bookmark.*

16. Select the **Event_Date** bookmark and in **Prompt** type **Enter the date of the next garden party**.

17. In **Default bookmark text**, type **the last Thursday of this month**. This will be added if the user doesn't type anything else. Check **Ask once** so that all the letters have the same response.

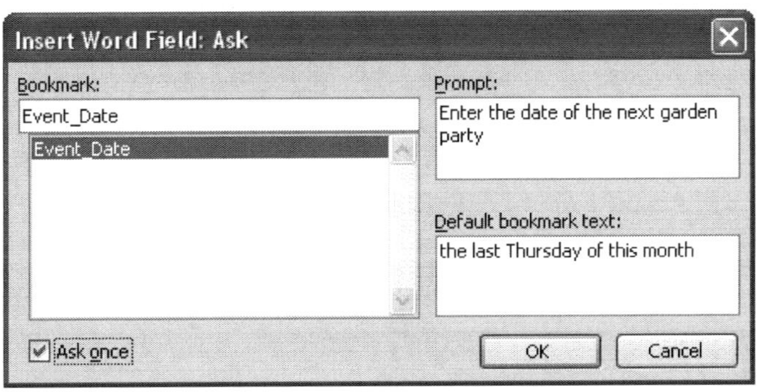

Driving Lesson 69 - Continued

18. Click **OK**, the **Ask** prompt is displayed click **OK** again. The result does not appear until a **Ref** field has been added.

19. Position the cursor at the bookmark location and select **Insert | Field** to display the **Field** dialog box.

20. Change the **Category** to **Links and References** and select **Ref** from the list.

21. From **Bookmark** name, select **Event_Date** and from the **Format** drop down select **Title case**.

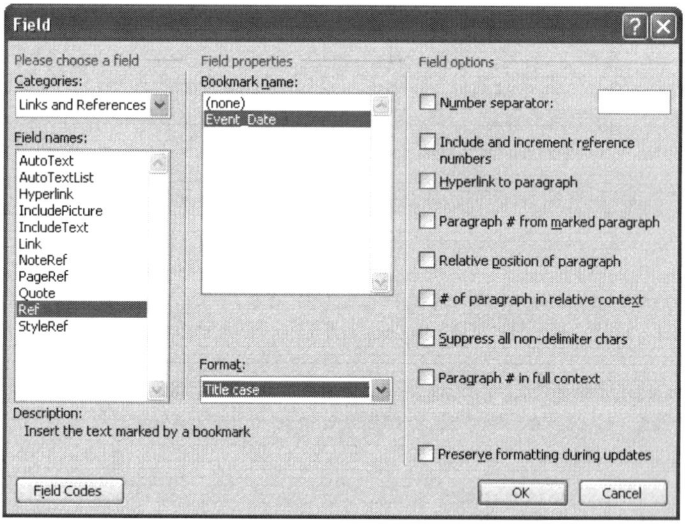

22. Click **OK**.

23. Use the **Mail Merge** task pane to complete the merge and the prompt will appear before printing or editing the merged letters.

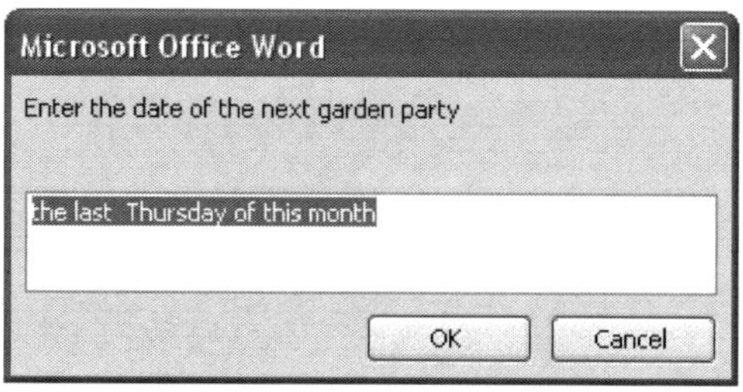

24. Type in **27th july** and click **OK**. The date is added to the letters. Check all the letters for the **Title case** date **27th July**.

25. Close any documents <u>without</u> saving.

Driving Lesson 70 - Revision: Mail Merge

This is not an ECDL test. Testing may only be carried out through certified ECDL test centres. This covers the features introduced in this section. Try not to refer to the preceding Driving Lessons while completing it.

1. Open the document **Conference**. This is a prepared mail merge letter, linked to a data source named **Clients**.
2. Locate the **Clients** data source from the files supplied and use the **Mail Merge Recipients** button, , to view the data form.
3. Change Aaron Dowson's company name to **Direct Pickles**.
4. In the **Mail Merge Recipients** dialog box, sort the records alphabetically by name.
5. Close **Conference** <u>without</u> saving.
6. Open **Conference** again.
7. To open a new data source – an *Access* database, select the **Conferences** database from the **Select Data Source** dialog box and the **No training** query from the **Select Table** dialog box.
8. Edit the main document, **Conference**, removing the original merge fields.
9. Insert the following fields in suitable positions:

    First Name

    Last Name

    Company

    Address1

    Address2

    City
10. Print the merged document.
11. Close **Conference** <u>without</u> saving.

If you experienced any difficulty completing this Revision refer back to the Driving Lessons in this section. Then redo the Revision.

Once you are confident with the features, complete the Record of Achievement Matrix referring to the section at the end of the guide. Only when competent move on to the next Section.

Section 12 Linking and Embedding

By the end of this Section you should be able to:

Link Data into a Document

Update and Break Links

Embed Data

Modify Embedded Data

To gain an understanding of the above features, work through the **Driving Lessons** in this **Section**.

For each **Driving Lesson**, read the **Park and Read** instructions, without touching the keyboard, then work through the numbered steps of the **Manoeuvres** on the computer. Complete the **Revision Exercise(s)** at the end of the section to test your knowledge.

Driving Lesson 71 - Linking Data

Park and Read

Documents can be **linked** to external data from a variety of other applications. Linking an object means that if its source data is changed, those changes can be reflected in the object. It also means that the source data can be opened directly from *Word*. Text from other documents, data and charts from spreadsheets can all be linked.

Manoeuvres

1. Start a new document and give it the heading **Puppy Facts**, **Arial**, **16pt**, **bold**, **centred**.

2. Text from another document is to be linked to this one. Position the cursor under the title and select **Insert | Object** and the **Create from File** tab.

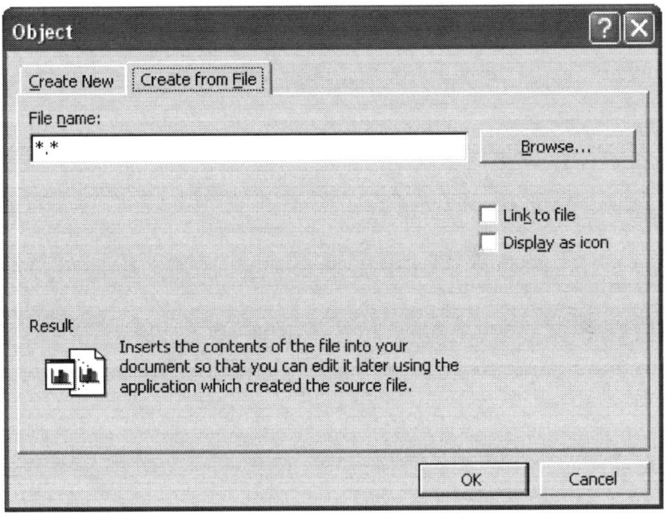

3. Browse for the data and select the **Puppy Info** document. Click **Insert**.

4. To ensure the file is linked, check **Link to file**. To display an icon rather than the whole document, check **Display as icon**. Click **OK**. The icon can be used to view the linked document, **Puppy Info**.

5. On a new line, a chart is to be inserted, showing numbers of registered breeders. Start a new line. Select **Insert | Object | Create from File** tab and this time insert the file **Pups.xls**. Check **Link to file** but do not check **Display as icon**. Click **OK**, this places the actual chart in the document.

6. Reduce the size of the linked chart to between the margins of the page.

7. Save the document as **Puppy Facts** and close it.

Driving Lesson 72 - Updating Links

Park and Read

Whenever a document containing links is opened, you will always be prompted to update the links. If the option is accepted, all linked objects within the document will be updated with the current versions from the source data. If not, they will be left unchanged.

Manoeuvres

1. Open the source file **Puppy Info**.
2. Delete the word **Labrador** in the first line and save and close the file.
3. Open the *Excel* file **Pups**.
4. Select the **Breeder Data** tab, if not already selected.
5. Change the value for **East** to **179**.
6. Select the **Breeder Ratios** tab to see the change.
7. Save and close the file. Close *Excel*.
8. Open the **Puppy Facts** document containing the links. The following prompt appears.

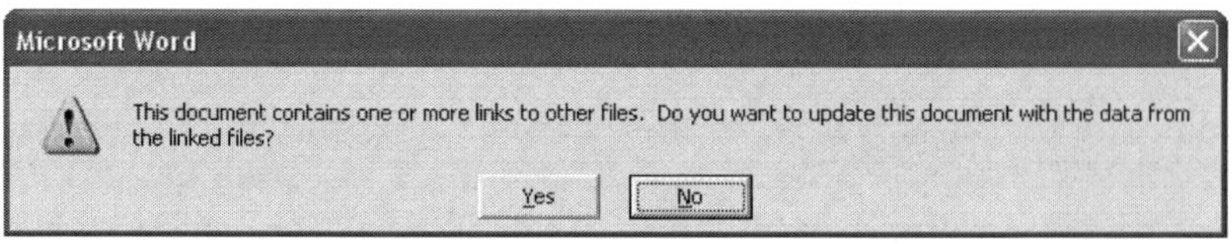

9. Select **Yes** to update the links. Notice the figure on the pie chart for **East** has changed to **179**.
10. Double click on the icon to open the linked *Word* document. The word **Labrador** is missing from the first line.
11. Close the **Puppy Info** document.
12. To break the link to the chart, select **Edit | Links**.

Driving Lesson 72 - Continued

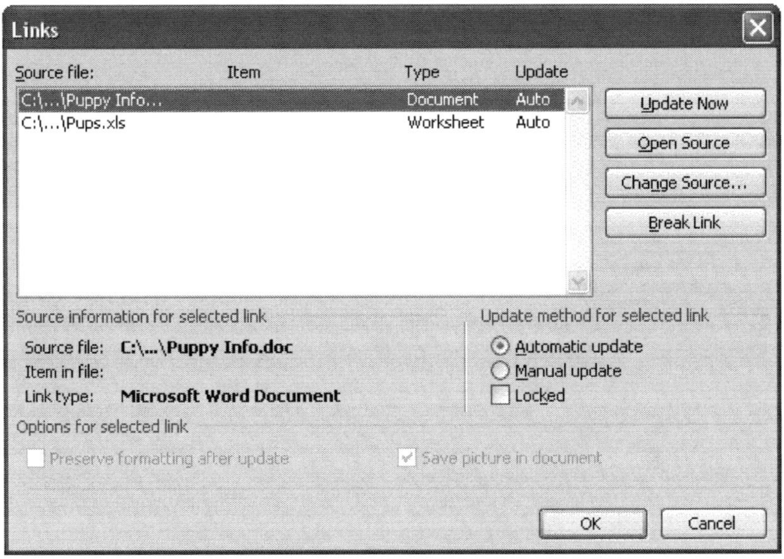

13. From the list, select the **Pups.xls** file and click **Break Link**.

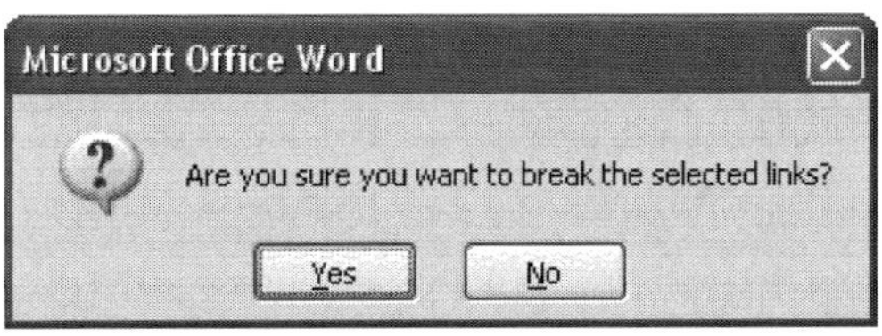

14. Select **Yes** at the prompt.
15. Click **OK** to close the **Links** dialog box.
16. Save and close **Puppy Facts**.
17. In *Excel* open **Pups** again and change the figure for **West** to **350** (**Breeder Data** tab). Check on the **Breeder Ratios** tab that the chart has been updated.
18. Save and close the file.
19. Reopen **Puppy Facts**, updating when prompted.
20. Notice that the figure for **West** remains at **238**, because the link has been broken.
21. Save the changes to **Puppy Facts** and leave it open.

Driving Lesson 73 - Embedding Data

Park and Read

When an object is **embedded** in a document, it will not change if the source file is amended. The default for inserting or pasting objects into a document is for them to be embedded. A linked object will be changed to an embedded object if the link is broken.

Manoeuvres

1. Using **Puppy Facts**, place the cursor beneath the pie chart.
2. In *Excel* open **Pups** and select the **Litters** tab. Save and close the file.
3. In **Puppy Facts**, select **Insert | Object | Create from File** and select **Pups.xls**.
4. Do not check **Link to file**.
5. Insert the file and resize it ensuring it's fully displayed.
6. Select **Edit | Links**. The chart is not shown, because it is embedded rather than linked.

If you copy a chart from Excel and paste it into a Word document it will also be embedded. However, you will not be able to edit the chart using this method. See next Driving Lesson.

7. Save the changes to the document and leave it open.

Driving Lesson 74 - Modifying Embedded Data

Park and Read

Embedded data can be updated manually from within *Word*. By double clicking on the embedded object, an editing mode is started, which allows you to make changes.

Manoeuvres

1. Double click on the embedded chart, **Litter Size Comparison** to activate the editing mode.
2. Click in cell **D4** and change the figure for **Ebony**'s **2002** litter to **10**.
3. Press <**Enter**>. Notice the figure and the chart have been updated.

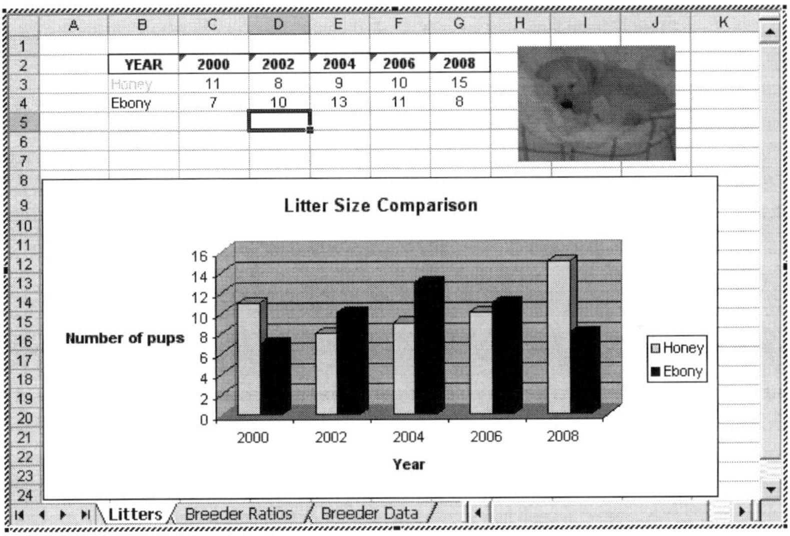

4. Click on the document area, away from the spreadsheet extract, to exit edit mode.

*The original chart in **Pups** has not been affected as this was embedded and not linked.*

5. Save the changes to the document.
6. Click on the embedded worksheet and with the handles displayed, press <**Delete**> to remove the embedded data.
7. Close the document <u>without</u> saving.
8. Close *Excel*.

Driving Lesson 75 - Revision: Linking and Embedding

This is not an ECDL test. Testing may only be carried out through certified ECDL test centres. This covers the features introduced in this section. Try not to refer to the preceding Driving Lessons while completing it.

1. Start a new document and link the *Excel* worksheet **Sales**.
2. Resize the linked object if necessary
3. Embed the chart from the worksheet beneath the spreadsheet extract in the document and resize it if necessary.
4. Save the document as **Regional Sales** and close it.
5. Open **Sales** in *Excel*.
6. On the **Sales** sheet, change the figure for **Central** in **June** to **£150,000**.
7. Save the file and close *Excel*.
8. Open the document **Regional Sales** and update the links. Notice the chart doesn't change.
9. Break the link to **Sales.xls**.
10. Save and close the **Regional Sales** document.

If you experienced any difficulty completing this Revision refer back to the Driving Lessons in this section. Then redo the Revision.

Once you are confident with the features, complete the Record of Achievement Matrix referring to the section at the end of the guide. Only when competent move on to the next Section.

Section 13 Macros

By the end of this Section you should be able to

Record a Macro

Run a Macro

Assign a Macro to a Button

To gain an understanding of the above features, work through the **Driving Lessons** in this **Section**.

For each **Driving Lesson**, read the **Park and Read** instructions, without touching the keyboard, then work through the numbered steps of the **Manoeuvres** on the computer. Complete the **Revision Exercise(s)** at the end of the section to test your knowledge.

Driving Lesson 76 - Recording a Macro

Park and Read

A **Macro** records keystrokes and menu selections, then plays them back exactly as they were recorded. A macro can be created so that a commonly used task can be performed, or a word, phrase or paragraph can be entered automatically. The use of macros results in the more efficient production of documents. Once macros have been created, they can be used at any time in any document that uses the same template.

A new macro can be created easily, but great care must be taken during the recording, because each action taken is incorporated into the macro.

Manoeuvres

1. Open a new document.
2. Select **Tools | Macro | Record New Macro**.
3. Enter the **Macro name** as **Landscape** and in **Description**, replace the text with **Change page setup**.

*Storing the macro in the **Normal** template means it will be available to in all documents. It is also possible to store macros with the current document only.*

4. Click **OK**. At this point the message **REC** is displayed in the **Status Bar** and the **Macro** toolbar is visible.

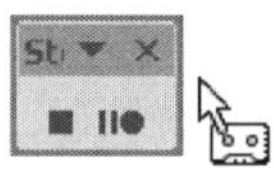

5. Notice how the mouse pointer has changed to a cassette tape, showing that the macro will now record all actions performed.

While recording a macro the mouse cannot be used at certain times, for example, when moving the insertion point around within the document or selecting text, the keyboard must be used.

6. Select **File | Page Setup | Margins** tab. Select **Landscape** from the **Orientation** section and click **OK**.
7. Select the **Stop Recording** button, ■, to end the recording.

*To record a macro quickly, double click **REC** on the **Status Bar** to display the **Record Macro** dialog box. Double click **REC** again to stop the macro recording.*

8. Close the document without saving.
9. A second macro will add fields to the headers and footers. Start a new document.

Driving Lesson 76 - Continued

10. Select **Tools | Macro | Record New Macro**. Name the macro **Footer** and click **OK**.

11. Select **View | Header and Footer** in the **Header** insert a field to add the file name and switch to the footer.

12. From the **Header and Footer** toolbar, select **Insert AutoText**. Click on **Author, Page #, Date**. This inserts the appropriate codes on the left, centre and right. (Any of the footer field options could be added here.)

13. Close the **Header and Footer** toolbar and **Stop** the macro. Close the document without saving.

14. A third macro will create a table that will repeat its header row over several pages. Start a new document.

15. Start a new macro called **TableHeader**. Use **Table | Insert | Table** and insert a table using the default setting, i.e. 5 columns and 2 rows. Enter **Monday**, **Tuesday**, **Wednesday**, etc., across the first row.

16. Select the first row using **Table | Select | Row** and centre and embolden the text.

In macro mode certain selections cannot be made via the mouse.

17. Select **Table | Table Properties | Row** tab and the option to **Repeat as header row at the top of each page**.

18. Click **Next Row**. In **Size** for Row 2, **Specify** a row height of **5 cm**, click **OK**, then **Stop** recording the macro.

19. From **Tools | Macro | Macros**, review the three created macros.

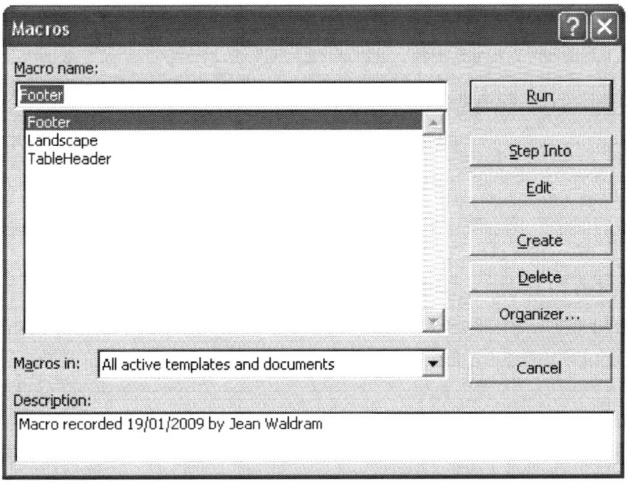

20. **Cancel** the dialog box and close all documents without saving.

Driving Lesson 77 - Running a Macro

Park and Read

Once a macro has been created and recorded, it can be run at any time.

Manoeuvres

1. Open the document **Summary**.
2. Select **Tools | Macro | Macros**.
3. From **Macros in**, select **All active templates and documents** and **Landscape** from the list.
4. Click **Run** to run the macro.
5. Print the document.
6. Close the document without saving.
7. Open **Discovery**. Use **File | Properties** to enter your name as the author. Click **OK**.
8. Select **Tools | Macro | Macros** and run the **Footer** macro.
9. Print Preview the document to ensure that the macro has used the correct information.
10. Close the document without saving.

Driving Lesson 78 - Assigning a Macro to a Button

Park and Read

The **Customize** dialog box can be used to assign a macro to a button on a toolbar. The button can then be added to any toolbar. The appearance of the button can also be changed. This can be done before or after the macro is recorded.

Manoeuvres

1. Start a new document and select **Tools | Customize**.
2. Click on the **Commands** tab and scroll down the list of **Categories** until **Macros** appears.
3. Click on **Macros** to view all the macros created.
4. Click and drag **Normal.NewMacros.TableHeader** up on to a toolbar. When the mouse is released a button appears.

5. Click on **Modify Selection** in the **Customize** dialog box and in the **Name** box, enter **Table**.

6. Click **Change Button Image**.

Driving Lesson 78 - Continued

7. Select the smiley face from the buttons.

8. Close the dialog box and click the button to run the macro.

9. To see the table header at work, press <**Tab**> until the table is large enough to cover two pages. Check that the header row is repeated.

10. Remove the button from the toolbar by holding <**Alt**> and dragging the button down off it.

11. To delete the macro, select **Tools | Macro | Macros**.

12. Select the **TableHeader** macro, then click **Delete**.

13. Select **Yes** at the prompt.

14. Delete the remaining macros and click **Close**.

15. Close the document without saving.

Driving Lesson 79 - Revision: Macros

This is not an ECDL test. Testing may only be carried out through certified ECDL test centres. This covers the features introduced in this section. Try not to refer to the preceding Driving Lessons while completing it.

1. Open the document **Stately Home**.
2. Create a new macro to print the current page of a document, using menu selections.
3. Name the macro **Page**.
4. Move to page 2 and run the **Page** macro.
5. Assign the macro to a button. Select the **eye** button.
6. Move to page 3 and run the macro using the new button.
7. Remove the button from the toolbar.
8. Delete the macro.
9. Close the document without saving.

If you experienced any difficulty completing this Revision refer back to the Driving Lessons in this section. Then redo the Revision.

Once you are confident with the features, complete the Record of Achievement Matrix referring to the section at the end of the guide.

Answers

Driving Lesson 5

Step 1 Purpose and audience.

Step 2 Spreadsheets, database tables for merge, images from libraries.

Step 3 Master document.

Step 4 Templates.

Step 5 Hyperlinks.

Step 6 **.txt** format.

Step 7 Web page.

Driving Lesson 12

Step 7 **Edit | Paste**.

Driving Lesson 14

Step 7 Only a single line is left at the top of the page. This is a widow.

Driving Lesson 32

Step 8 S Westgarth is last on the list.

Driving Lesson 50

Step 10 **Original Showing Markup**.

Glossary

AutoText	A tool that inserts pre-stored phrases or graphics to text, avoiding repetitive keyboard entries.
Bookmark	A named location or selection of text, which can then be used for reference purposes or searching.
Caption	A numbered label that can be added to various types of object within a document. The numbering can be automatic.
Comment	A note added to a specific location or selected text within a document that is displayed as a **ScreenTip** above the associated text.
Cross-reference	Used to refer to an item elsewhere in a document.
Data Source	A file containing records, that can be merged with a main document. This file may be a document, database or spreadsheet.
Endnote	A piece of text that is placed at the end of a document, giving further information about a text entry or object within it. Numbers are automatically placed within the document, next to the text to be referenced and the note text.
Field	A placeholder within a document that contains a field code, which inserts current information, e.g. page number, date, etc.
Field Code	The instructions within a field that generate the information to be inserted.
Footnote	A piece of text that is placed at the foot of a page, giving further information about a text entry or object on that page. Numbers are automatically placed within the document, next to the text to be referenced and the note text.
Indent	A measurement by which text is moved away from either the left or right margin.
Justified	An alignment setting that provides straight margins at both left and right.
Mail Merge	A facility that combines a main document with records held within a data source.
Main Document	A document containing merge fields, where information from a data source is to be inserted.

Master Document	A document that is made up of a number of separate files or sub-documents.
Object	An item imported or created, e.g. picture, drawing, chart.
Orphan	The first line of a paragraph that is separated from the rest and left at the bottom of the current page.
Outline	A view of the document that displays the hierarchy of styles used within it.
Password to Modify	A level of protection that allows a document to be opened and altered, but modifications can only be saved if a new file name is used.
ScreenTip	Notes that appear in yellow boxes, giving extra information about specific text or objects within a document. They are usually displayed when the cursor is positioned or clicked over the appropriate location.
Section	Part of a document that is to be formatted differently from the rest e.g. page numbering or layout. Created by section breaks.
Style	Pre-created combinations of formatting, consisting of paragraph and font formats.
Sub-document	A document that is a component part of a master document. Sub-documents may be opened and edited individually, but remain linked to the master document.
Template	A base document that contains elements of formatting and alignment and that can be used over and over again.
Text Orientation	The formatting that determines whether text reads horizontally or vertically on the page.
Text Wrapping	The formatting that determines how text flows (wraps) around inserted objects such as graphics.
Tracking	A feature that makes it possible to see where and when changes were made to a document and who made them.
Watermark	An object (which may be a text box) that is placed on the background of a page, so that text appears over the top of it.
Widow	The final line of a paragraph that is separated from the rest and printed at the top of a new page.
WordArt	A graphical text feature. **WordArt** is manipulated in the same way as other objects.

Index

Record of Achievement Matrix

This Matrix is to be used to measure your progress while working through the guide. This is a learning reinforcement process, you judge when you are competent.

Tick boxes are provided for each feature. 1 is for no knowledge, 2 some knowledge and 3 is for competent. A section is only complete when column 3 is completed for all parts of the section.

For details on sitting ECDL Examinations in your country please contact the local ECDL Licensee or visit the European Computer Driving Licence Foundation Limited web site at http://www.ecdl.org.

Tick the Relevant Boxes **1**: No Knowledge **2**: Some Knowledge **3**: Competent

Section	No.	Driving Lesson	1	2	3
1 Working Efficiently	1	Design			
	2	Techniques			
	3	Hyperlinks			
	4	Saving			
2 Text Editing	6	Find and Replace			
	7	Paste Special Options			
	8	AutoCorrect			
	9	AutoFormat			
	10	AutoText			
	11	Text Flow and Wrap			
3 Paragraph Editing	13	Line Spacing			
	14	Pagination Options			
	15	Creating Styles			
	16	Modifying Styles			
	17	Outline Level Styles			
	18	Multilevel Lists			
4 Document Setup	20	Adding/Deleting Section Breaks			
	21	Applying Section Formatting			
	22	Section Headers and Footers			
	23	Multiple Column Layout			
	24	Modifying Column Layout			
	25	Modifying Column Width/Spacing			
	26	Creating a Watermark			
	27	Modifying and Deleting Watermarks			
5 Tables	29	Table AutoFormat			
	30	Merging a Splitting Cells			
	31	Converting Text to Table			
	32	Sorting Table Data			
	33	Performing Calculations			
	34	Table Properties and Setup			

Tick the Relevant Boxes **1**: No Knowledge **2**: Some Knowledge **3**: Competent

Section	No.	Driving Lesson	1	2	3
6 Referencing	36	Creating Footnotes and Endnotes			
	37	Modifying/Deleting Footnotes/Endnotes			
	38	Creating a Table of Contents			
	39	Updating a Table of Contents			
	40	Adding and Deleting Bookmarks			
	41	Cross-Referencing			
	42	Adding Numbered Captions			
	43	Creating a Table of Figures			
	44	Creating an Index			
7 Collaborative Editing	46	Adding/Editing Comments			
	47	Tracking Changes			
	48	Accept/Rejecting Changes			
	49	Compare and Merge			
8 Document Security	51	Password Protection			
	52	Removing/Changing Passwords			
9 Master Documents and Templates	54	Creating a Master Document			
	55	Creating a Subdocument			
	56	Adding/Removing Subdocument			
	57	Modifying a Template			
10 Field Codes and Forms	59	Working with Field Codes			
	60	Editing and Updating Field Codes			
	61	Locking/Unlocking Fields			
	62	Creating and Editing Forms			
	63	Form Field Options			
	64	Protecting Form Fields			
11 Mail Merge	66	Editing a Data Source			
	67	Sorting a Data Source			
	68	Using Various Data Sources			
	69	ASK and IF Fields			
12 Linking and Embedding	71	Linking Data			
	72	Updating Links			
	73	Embedding Data			
	74	Modifying Embedded Data			
13 Macros	76	Recording a Macro			
	77	Running a Macro			
	78	Assigning a Macro to a Button			

Other Products from CiA Training Ltd

CiA Training Ltd is a leading publishing company, which has consistently delivered the highest quality products since 1985. A wide range of flexible and easy to use self teach resources has been developed by CiA's experienced publishing team to aid the learning process. These include the following ECDL Foundation approved products at the time of publication of this product:

- **ECDL/ICDL Syllabus 5.0**
- **ECDL/ICDL Advanced Syllabus 2.0**
- **ECDL/ICDL Revision Series**
- **ECDL/ICDL Advanced Syllabus 2.0 Revision Series**
- **e-Citizen**

Previous syllabus versions also available - contact us for further details.

We hope you have enjoyed using our materials and would love to hear your opinions about them. If you'd like to give us some feedback, please go to:

www.ciatraining.co.uk/feedback.php

and let us know what you think.

New products are constantly being developed. For up to the minute information on our products, to view our full range, to find out more, or to be added to our mailing list, visit:

www.ciatraining.co.uk